CHRIST AND THE JEWS

CORNELIUS VAN TIL

**THE PRESBYTERIAN AND REFORMED
PUBLISHING COMPANY**

1968

International Library of Philosophy and Theology
Biblical And Theological Studies
Robert L. Reymond, *Editor*

Library of Congress Card Catalogue Number 68-25835
Printed in the United States of America

CONTENTS

EDITOR'S PREFACE

The Jew is an enigma both to the world at large and to the Christian man. The world has never known quite how to take or "what to do" with the Jew. But do something it has always felt it must. Throughout her history in Old Testament times, Israel found herself occasionally envied for her cultural and political attainments, but more often the brunt of alien military pounding as foreign powers swept back and forth between Mesopotamia and Egypt. The Northern Kingdom finally suffered defeat at the hand of Assyria in 722 B. C.; the Southern Kingdom fared little better, falling to the Neo-Babylonians in 586 B. C. After their captivity in Babylon, the returned remnant established the Second Commonwealth, only to know once again the ravages of war during the Hasmonean Period and subjugation to Imperial Rome. In A. D. 70, Jerusalem, the center of Jewish worship since the time of King David, was razed to the ground by Roman armies under Titus. And from that day until the recent Six Days' War, Jerusalem was trodden under foot by the Gentiles. It was only in recent times (1948) that there even existed a national homeland for the Jew, and at times even its security has been in doubt. In short, the Jews of the Diaspora, the Jews of the European ghettos, indeed, *world* Jewry, have in every walk and clime been regarded as aliens. And yet the Jew is still with us. It would seem that He who keeps Israel, indeed, neither slumbers nor sleeps!

This very fact poses a genuine problem for the Christian man. What should his attitude be toward these people through whom came his Old Testament, his Savior according to the flesh, indeed, his very salvation (John 4:22)? Should it not be one of admiration and gratitude? Should he not do everything in his power to make the lot of the Jew more acceptable? And yet have not the Jews rejected

iii

his Savior and Lord, declaring Him to be only one of a long line of prophets and messiahs but definitely not the Son of God, definitely not God manifest in human flesh for redemptive purposes? And do not the Jews regard the Christian himself as an idolater?

Some Christians, taking quite seriously the Lord's statement in Genesis 12:3, "I will bless them that bless thee [Abraham], and him that curseth thee will I curse," feel quite strongly that they should definitely befriend the Jew and aid him in his political drive for national independence and his religious drive for idealogical freedom. At least, he should rejoice with his Jewish friend when progress in these areas is made.

Now while no Christian worthy of that name would advocate anything in the least way resembling violence toward or discrimination against the Jew because of his nationality or religion, nonetheless, it does seem a very real betrayal of his Lord, who has suffered much at Jewish (and Gentile) hands, both physically at the time of his first advent and idealogically through the centuries since that time, for the Christian man to encourage or to support in any way the Jew in the maintenance of his national and religious "Jewishness." In no uncertain terms, Paul denounced *every* Jewish hope for acceptability before God which is founded on anything other than the righteousness of Christ imputed to man and received by faith alone. Racial connection with Abraham or Moses counts for nought (Rom. 9:7-8). A righteousness borne out of good works and the keeping of the law is futile (Gal. 2: 16). Even the highest and best of Jewish extra-Biblical tradition only makes void the true Word of God (Mk. 7:13). Paul was convinced that by their rejection of Jesus the Christ, "his kinsmen according to the flesh" had called down upon themselves the wrath of God *eis telos* (I Thes. 2:14-16). And he was equally convinced that the Jew must give up that very distinctive which separates him from other men, namely, his exalted idea of his own acceptability before God because of his racial relation to the Patriarchs and his obedience to the Torah, if he is ever to know genuine conversion to God through repentance and faith in Jesus Christ. It is indeed a strange twist of thinking, if not outright treason, for the Christian man in any way to aid or to abet the Jew in his retention of that distinctive, the holding on to which only solidifies him in his unbelief. And yet, in order that the blessing of Genesis 12:3 might be his, and in order that he might escape

iv

the promised curse of the same verse, many an untrained Christian blindly encourages the Jew in his "Jewishness," failing to realize that as long as the Jew continues to practice his Judaism, just so long will he continue to reject Him who is the Hope of Israel.

Again, one is often told by "authorities" who should know better that in his witness to Jewish friends the Christian may assume that the one to whom he is witnessing already believes the Old Testament scriptures, and it only remains to show him that Christ Jesus is the one whom the prophets foresaw. But what betrayal this is on the part of the Christian! As if one could *believe* the Old Testament and not see Jesus Christ as Messiah, Savior, and Lord revealed therein! The real truth of the matter is that no Jew who has heard of Christ and his atoning work and who rejects him believes the Old Testament. Jesus expressly declared to the Jews of his day: "If ye believed Moses, ye would believe me; for he wrote of me" (Jn. 5:46).

The Christian should love the Jew, certainly. But the sooner the Christian realizes that the Jew is as hopelessly lost and as hopelessly blind, if not more so (Rom. 11:6-11), than the Gentile, and that to win the Jew to Christ he must crush any and every hope for salvation which is related in any way to the fact that he is a Jew and a "son of the Torah," the sooner the Christian will honor his Lord by his witness to the Jew and the more effective will his witness become.

Recognizing all this, in this monograph the author clearly sets ancient and modern Jewish thought over against Christian thought and demonstrates that there can only be opposition between them when both are advocated from the standpoint of their respective "standards" and presuppositions. Moreover, he shows that when modern Protestantism denies the infallible revelation of God in Jesus Christ and in the Old and New Testaments, it thereby loses all opportunity to convert the Jew to Christianity and even joins the Jewish apologist in the latter's avowed disdain for the Christ of Protestant Orthodoxy.

It is with genuine concern for the salvation of the Jews that the Presbyterian and Reformed Publishing Company releases this work. The Christian who is concerned that his witness to the Jew be scripturally sound and honoring to his Lord will receive help and have his offensive "spiritual weapons" sharpened by the reading of *Christ and the Jews*.

ROBERT L. REYMOND

v

INTRODUCTION

Modern Jews have a life-and-world view through which they seek to become a blessing to the world. This life-and-world view has no place in it for Christ. The Jews believe that men can know and serve the true God and therein be "saved" only if they reject the claims of Christ.

When a Christian worships Christ as the Son of God he is, says the Jew, an idolater. And he sees his mission as that of bringing such an idol-worshiper back to the God of Abraham and of Moses.

In seeking to fulfill his mission in relation to Christian idolaters the Jew must, of course, *oppose* the claims of Christ. Even so, his ultimate aim is *positive*. It is to win the Christian to the service of the one true God.

Martin Buber speaks of Jesus as "a great Son of Israel." [1] He says that "in the teaching of Jesus himself, as we know it from the early texts of the gospels, the genuinely Jewish principle is manifest." [2] He adds: "From my youth onwards, I have found in Jesus my great brother." [3]

It would seem that Buber's position is quite different from that of the Pharisees in Jesus' day. But is this really so? Is it not rather true that according to Buber the "genuinely Jewish principle" has already won the battle. The Jews brought true monotheism into the world. Christians will now gladly follow their lead to the one God, the God beyond any and every form of human knowledge. The only Christians who need to be opposed today are those who still think that in Christ and in the Bible as his Word there is a direct and final revelation of the true God to man in history. All the rest already worship the true God. All the rest are in the kingdom of God, and even the "fundamentalist" will some day be.

Our main purpose in this brief monograph on Jewish Apologetics is, in turn, to understand and to evaluate the position of the modern Jew in order to win him to Christ. The historical mission of the

1

Jews was to bring forth Jesus as Christ in order that through him the world, Jew and Gentile alike, might be saved. When Buber speaks of Jesus as his "great brother" without speaking of him as his divine Savior, this is still to reject Christ. And with the rejection of Christ by the Jew his mission in history dissipates as the waters of a river in a desert. But Christ will not allow the Jew thus to defeat himself in rejecting him. Through his Spirit Christ can and will create a new heart within him and give him true repentance toward him. Then, together with all Gentiles who truly repent, all Israel shall be saved.

NOTES

1. Martin Buber, *Two Types of Faith* (tr. Norman P. Goldhawk; New York: Harper & Brothers, 1961), p. 9.
2. *Ibid.*, p. 12.
3. *Ibid.*

CHAPTER I

PHILO JUDAEUS

Judaism thinks of itself as having received from the one and only true God the task of making him known to all men everywhere. The one and only true God, the Jews insist, has revealed himself to Israel, and more particularly to Moses, in order through them to make known his way of life to them and to all mankind. All men must be instructed in the wisdom of the Torah; only if they know and heed this wisdom can they be saved.

The opportunity to fulfill this God-given task opened up to the Jews as never before at the beginning of the common era. Even before this time there had been some measure of contact between Judaism and Hellenism. But now there was in Alexandria a great center of Hellenistic culture. And there were also large colonies of Jews living in Alexandria.

One of these Jews had been thoroughly trained in all that Hellenism stood for in his day. Yet he was a true Jew. He was a missionary Jew. He was not a mere eclectic. He did not seek for a synthesis between Judaism and Greek culture by thinking of them as having equal rights to claim the loyalties of good men. James Drummond assures us of this when he says of Philo: "He did not intend to step into the arena as the champion of a new philosophy, but rather to present an *apologia* for the teaching of Moses by showing that, even when it appeared questionable or trifling, it was full of the highest philosophical truth. His philosophy, therefore, only comes by the way of, and is guided by, the requirements of his biblical interpretation.[1]

The reader of Philo may doubt that his philosophy is really "guided by the requirements of his biblical interpretation." Does he not seem to engage in the study of philosophy for its own sake? Does he not, as did the Greeks, simply start from human experience

3

as intelligible in itself without any reference to the revelation given by the one true God to Moses alone?

The solution would seem to lie in the fact that all men everywhere can, according to Philo, prove to themselves the *fact* of God's existence but that only by revelation can they know something of the *nature* of God's being. *That* God exists could be and had been established by philosophy, but *what* God is they must learn from Moses.

But this distinction between the *that* and the *what* as they pertain to God is obviously not a wholly satisfactory one. Can we simply say, and does Philo simply say, that by *reason,* that is, by philosophy, men can prove *that* God exists and that by *faith* alone men can know *what* God's nature is? The answer must be in the negative. To prove *that* God exists without knowing *anything* of his nature is an unintelligible procedure. It would be the equivalent of proving the existence of a zero, the existence of a being who is completely interchangeable with non-being.

Then too, Philo does, as a matter of fact, prove something about the nature of God. He proves to us that God is not the kind of God in which the Epicureans believed. He proves, beyond this, that Plato has given us a better description of the nature of God than did Aristotle or the Stoics.

Moreover, Philo proves the existence of God from a study of the nature of the world and of man. And the nature of man, Philo finds, gives clearer proof of the existence of God than does the nature of the world.

Still further, if we must start our search for the existence of God from a study of the nature of man, then we must find the nature of man not in the lower but in the higher aspect of his being. If the cosmos as a whole is for Philo, as Drummond summarizes him, "a tissue of rational force, which images the beauty, the power, the goodness of its primeval fountain," then "the reason of man is this same rational force entering into consciousness. . . ." [2] This reason of man then is Philo's primary starting point. He traces back the nature of this reason to the idea of the Logos.

Of particular interest to us is the fact that, according to Philo, man's "rules of conduct" are to be the natural expression of his reason, and it is as an expression of the Logos that the human reason must guide man's conduct. Thus it is that God confronts us through the mediation of the Logos. "From first to last the Logos is the Thought of God, dwelling subjectively in the infinite Mind, planted out and made objective in the universe." [3] Wherever we turn we meet the thoughts or words or works of God. It is thus by observing the world and chiefly our own rational nature that we are told of that "impenetrable *Being* from whose inexhaustible fulness" proceeds "that uniting and cosmic Thought" in which we all live and move and have our being.[4]

There are certain problems that now press upon us in connection with Philo's starting point.

First, there is the question of the internal relation between the assertions of reason with respect of God. Can reason say that God is indescribable because wholly beyond all the categories of human thought, and then at once undertake to describe him by these self-same categories?

Drummond says that, according to Philo, the world and man both *suggest* and *veil* the existence of God.[5] And so far as Philo thinks in terms of Greek philosophy, this faces him with a great difficulty.

The Greeks assumed that the mind of man participates in the mind of God. Together with all other men fallen in Adam, they sought to suppress the fact that they were creatures of God. They took for granted that if man is to know anything he must know it in the way that God knows it, namely, exhaustively. Parmenides gave striking expression to this notion of man's knowledge as participant in God's knowledge when he said that only that *can* exist which man can, without contradiction, say *must* exist. Accordingly all being must, according to Parmenides, be eternal or changeless being. If then man is to have any knowledge, he must be one with that eternal being. This amounts to saying that if he is to know, it is not he who knows but it is God who knows in him. On this basis only God knows God. Moreover, on this basis there is nothing that exists besides God. Therefore, only God knows and there is nothing that God can know beside himself. Thus Truth and Being are not really *beyond* man. It is rather that there is no man distinct from God. If we speak of any distinction between God and man we do so figuratively rather than intellectually.

Of course, the Greeks did speak of man as somehow distinct from God. But when they sought for a reason that could justify

5

them in doing so they found none. They had to resort, therefore, to the notion of a non-rational principle as the source of their own individual existence. Since they reduced God to a pure or abstract Form utterly above and negatively related to the world they were compelled to postulate the idea of pure or abstract matter as the correlative to this God as pure Form.

One point more must here be made. It is to the effect that on this Greek view, the idea of the Good is identical with the idea of Truth and of Being. Ethics, as well as epistemology and metaphysics, is, on this Greek basis, constructed on this Form-Matter scheme.

There were, of course, many differences of detail between the various Greek philosophers. And the fact that there are these differences opens up an almost endless opportunity for Philo scholars. Did Philo's view of God resemble that of the Stoics? There are Stoic elements in Philo, we are told. Did his view of God resemble that of Aristotle? Again, there are Aristotelian elements in Philo, we are told. But Philo's God chiefly resembles the God of the Pythagoreans and of Plato.

Again, does Philo's method of reasoning by which he seeks to establish the existence of God resemble most the method of Stoicism, the method of Aristotle, or the method of Plato? Again, it is Plato rather than Aristotle or the Stoics who seems to dominate Philo.

Harry Austryn Wolfson says that "the starting point of Philo's philosophy is the theory of ideas."[6] And this theory, says Wolfson, "was with him a philosophic inheritance from Plato."[7] Moreover, Philo, like Plato, uses the *ideas* as patterns of things in the world.[8] Thus, however much Philo may modify the theory of ideas, his inspiration in dealing with it is Platonic.

If Philo agrees more with Plato than with any other Greek philosopher as to the nature of God, the same is true, argues Wolfson, with respect to the proofs for the existence of God. In his *Timæus* Plato used the causal argument for the existence of God. Philo follows Plato on this point.[9] Philo argues that "even on the Aristotelian assumption of the eternity of the world there is proof for the existence of a god who as the immovable mover of the world is also the cause of its existence."[10] As for what was later called the teleological argument, it already had in Philo's time "a long tradition dating back to Plato, the early writing of Aristotle, and the Stoics."[11]

6

We may agree with Wolfson that both in his view of the nature of God and in his view of the proper way of proving the existence of God, Philo is more Platonic than Aristotelian or Stoic. Even so, the main point to observe for our purpose is that the Form-Matter scheme is present everywhere in Greek philosophy.

Herman Dooyerweerd traces the development of this scheme in great detail and finds its climactic expression in Aristotle. And it is this Form-Matter scheme that Philo uses in his philosophical arguments with respect both to the nature of God and to the method of proving his exisence.

I. The Unknowability of God

Philo maintains that God cannot be known "according to His essence" by any creature.[12] According to Philo, God is unnamable *akatonomastou,* ineffable, *arrytou,* and "in every way incomprehensible *akatalyptou.*" [13]

Did Philo derive this notion of the wholly unknowable God from the Greeks, and more specifically, from Plato? Wolfson thinks not. Says he: "Now neither Plato nor Aristotle definitely says that God according to His essence cannot be known or is incomprehensible or cannot be envisaged even in mind." [14] He adds: "Nor is the conception of the ineffability or unnamability of God found in any other Greek philosopher before Philo." [15]

Having said this, Wolfson undertakes a refutation of E. Norden's argument with respect to this matter as found in the work on the *Agnostos Theos.*[16]

When the apostle Paul speaks in Acts 17:23 of the altar to the unknown God, says Wolfson, Norden takes this to refer to an "unknowable God," that is to say, "to a God that by His nature cannot be known." [17]

And on what does Norden base his contention? He bases it first on the fact that the Greeks speak of God as invisible and incomprehensible. But by speaking of God in this way the Greeks meant only to deny "that God can be seen or comprehended by the senses; they do not say that God's essence cannot be comprehended by the mind." [18] Second, Norden refers to a fragment of Heraclitus. Heraclitus speaks of men who pray to images "as if one were to talk with a man's house, knowing not what gods or heroes are." [19]

7

But these vague words of Heraclitus seem only to indicate, says Wolfson, that as to the gods men must depend upon hearsay rather than observation.

Where then did Philo get his notion of the unnamable God? From the Old Testament, says Wolfson. He quotes Exodus 33:23 where we read that "Moses went into thick darkness, where God was" and God says to Moses: "Thou shalt see what is behind Me, but My face thou shalt not see." "From these verses he infers that God 'by His very nature cannot be seen,' by which he means that God cannot be comprehended by the mind. Once he has established the incomprehensibility of God by these verses, he derives therefrom the impossibility of naming God, for 'it is a logical consequence that no proper name even can be appropriately assigned to the truly existent,' and in proof of this he says: 'Note that when the prophet desires to know what he must answer to those who ask about His name He says "I am He that is," which is equivalent to "My nature is to be, not to be spoken."' Another proof-text quoted by him is the verse 'I appeared to Abraham, Isaac and Jacob as their God, but my name Lord I did not reveal to them.' And once he has established the unnamability of God by these verses, he derives therefrom the incomprehensibility of God, arguing that 'indeed, if He is unnamable, He is also inconceivable and incomprehensible.' " [20]

What shall we say about all this? We may, possibly, doubt whether Philo thought of Plato as teaching the idea of the unknown God, but we cannot doubt that he thought he found this doctrine in the Old Testament. Nor can we doubt that, according to Philo, a true philosophy also teaches this doctrine. Philo asserts that reason and revelation are in full harmony on this point.

In contradistinction from Philo we would maintain that "reason" and revelation stand in complete opposition on this. "Reason" as understood by Greek philosophy assumes, even if it does not verbally teach, the utter unknowability of God. The "reason" of the Greeks is the reason of apostate man. And apostate man has every reason for teaching the unnamability of God. If God is unnamable then he cannot name anything in the world. Only if God is unknowable can man think of his own knowledge as autonomous.

But God, who at the beginning named all things that he had created, would not allow his name to be blotted out by the creature who refused to be named by God. He sent his Son, the full expression of his substance, to speak out his name among sinful men. This Son allowed his name to be blotted out on the cross in order thus to rename a people in his own name. He sent his servant Moses to speak forth his name for him. Having appeared in grace to Moses, he gave his law to be a teacher of his name.

While the Greeks, together with, and in a sense leading, all apostate mankind, insisted that to know the name of God man must know him exhaustively, they knew not at all this self-naming God through his self-naming Son, who appeared to Moses to instruct him as to the proper naming of all things. But Philo, not knowing this self-naming Son of God, reduces his revelation through Moses to an identity with the "revelation" of the nameless God of apostate philosophy. Philo virtually reduced the revelation of God in his Son through Moses to a God-projection such as Plato had made. Moses and Plato are forced to be friends with one another in their common opposition to Christ. Thus men love darkness rather than light. The Son of God came unto his own and his own received him not.

II. A Negative Mystical Theology

The doctrine of the unnamable God as taught by Philo may be spoken of as negative theology. But negative theology is meaningless theology. Man cannot speak of God unless God first speaks of himself to man. But in negative theology he cannot speak to man, For there is no man distinct from himself to whom he may speak. For man, to be man at all, must, on the view of Philo, be one with God.

Negative theology implies mystical theology and mystical theology implies negative theology. According to Philo, the rational power within us as men "is our sovereign part." [21] "Mind is in its whole genus superior to sensible perception, as man is to woman; for it is known by its activity, but the senses, like woman, are characterized by susceptibility, being altogether dependent upon external objects." [22]

The rational soul then issues laws and customs to the irrational soul. But in doing so, the rational soul thinks back to its participation in deity. For "as Moses was a god to Pharoah, so mind is a god to the irrational soul, and is for everyone his peculiar divinity." [23]

9

Thus Philo reaches up into his unnamable God by the internal sense of man. He also argues that we reason from the nature of the world to God. But if the knowledge of the world is obtained by sense-experience and sense-experience is purely receptive, then this knowledge of the world is dependent upon the knowledge man has by virtue of his rational principle which is active. But then this rational principle is made to depend upon God. Man's knowledge is true because it participates in divine knowledge. But man, so far as he is man, knows nothing of this divine knowledge. Man knows himself only to the extent that he is participant in divinity. But then so far as he is participant in divinity he is participant in the unnamable or unknowable God.

III. Logos Theology

But let us see if we can get out of this dilemma by means of the Logos idea. By mystical absorption we work from man up to God. By logos theology we work down from God to man. Surely man is a derivative being. How could we start from him unless we already know him through God as underivative being? [24] We must, it is said, by all means have a univocal point of contact between man and God. If there is no commonality of attributes between God and man, how can we know either? But if we have commonality of attributes, then we are in a common distress. Man's rational principle is said to be the governing principle. But what does it govern? Chaos? Man's rational principle can only govern his "irrational principle" if God governs both. Man needs a transcendent God or his rational principle is merely correlative to his irrational principle. Man needs a *wholly* transcendent God, one who is in nowise correlative to an irrational principle, either in himself or in man, or he can be of no help to man. But when he becomes *wholly* transcendent to man, then there is no longer any univocal element between them.

But the Logos idea will cure all this, will it not? If we cannot reach to a *wholly* other God by reasoning *von unten* let us try it by reasoning *von oben*. The Logos comes to us from God. He, or it, reveals God. Reveals God? How can we be certain that it is *God* that he reveals? Surely he must be *wholly* revealed or he is not revealed at all. And unless he is *wholly* revealed we cannot know

10

that it is God that is revealed. But if he is wholly revealed then he is *wholly* identical with us and is, in no sense, transcendent above us.

The term Logos, says Wolfson, is "used by Philo in the sense of *Nous,* both as the mind of God which is identical with His essence and as a created mind which is distinct from His essence. . . ." [25]

The Logos then is for Philo the Mediator between God and man. He is sent from above. But since it is the unknowable God who sends him he is himself unknowable. Or if he is in any sense knowable then it is not God who has sent him.

Is the world made by the Logos? Is that why the world is a tissue of rationality? But if the world is made by the Logos then this world must be wholly rational to man. Then *evil* too must proceed from the Logos. Then prophecy and miracles are predictable. But if we must have a theodicy, if we must not implicate God in evil, then we must cut him off from the world. Then God must be neither the creator nor the providential controller of the world.

Perhaps the solution to all these problems, every one of them springing from the assumption that Greek philosophy is right in its assumption of human autonomy, can be found in the principle of dialecticism.

IV. Allegorical Theology

If we are to try out the principle of dialecticism as a possible solution to our question of man and his environment, then we must first demythologize the Old Testament. Philo had not heard of this word, nor did he speak of dialecticism. Philo accomplished what modern dialecticism accomplishes by means of *Entmythologisierung* by the help of allegory.

By means of allegorization Philo rescued the revelation of God in the Old Testament (and more particularly the revelation of God through Moses) from its literalism and from the obscurantism that goes with it. By means of allegorization Philo lifted Moses out of the I-it dimension to that of person-to-person confrontation. By means of allegorization Philo shows that the Torah is not something externally given to man but that it proceeds, as all truly ethical law must proceed, from the ethical consciousness of man. Allegorical interpretation reduces the convenantal revelation of God through

11

Christ to Israel to a rationalist-mysticist mythology. It is thus by his allegorization that Philo misdirects the stream of redemptive revelation found in the Old Testament so that it does not culminate in Christ to the fructification of mankind but is lost in the desert of apostate thought and life.

To be sure, the form of apostate thought with which Philo identifies Christ's revelation of himself in the Old Testament is that of a high spiritualism and a noble ethicism over against all form of materialism. Philo advocates a high personalist philosophy against all forms of impersonalism. As Plato and Aristotle, following Socrates, sought for a teleological and therefore an ethical interpretation of the world of man, so Philo, following them and reducing the Torah to a natural law in the spiritual world, opposes every lower view of life. In Philo Hellenism and Judaism together stand for the primacy of personality and practical reason as over against the hard-shelled sceptics, rationalists, and empiricists.

An abundance of evidence found in Philo to prove the point just made may be found summarized in Edwin R. Goodenough's work *By Light, Light*.[26] Only a few details can be mentioned here. The most convenient way of setting out even some of this evidence is to follow Goodenough in his argument.

V. The God of Mystery

"One of the most familiar facts," says Goodenough, "about Philo is that to him God was the Absolute, a single and unique Being beyond even the Monad and the number One, as well as beyond the Good and all other categories. Yet, like the God of later Neo-Platonism, Philo's Deity had somehow to be brought into relation with the world, in spite of the fact that He was essentially beyond relation. In the solution of the problem of how the unrelated God could be the God of the universe Philo vividly foreshadows the thought of Plotinus. The sun was taken as the figure, that orb which burns, to all appearances, eternally, yet without need of fuel from outside itself. Independent of the world, a self-sufficient existence, it sends out its great stream of light and heat which makes life possible upon the earth. This stream may be called a stream of light, or of heat, or of life, or of creation. But the stream itself is greater than any of these single aspects, since it includes them all.

12

The aspects are only convenient abstractions for our immediate purpose, for the stream from the sum is not a pluralistic collection of independent elements, but is itself a unit." [27]

Of course, says Goodenough, "the figure of light was definitely always a figure of speech rather than a literal transference of the details of ancient physical theories of light." [28]

Philo finds the Old Testament teaching essentially the same thing that he finds taught in the philosophical schools as they go on their way from Plato to Plotinus.

Man is to be saved by being raised up in the scale of being, to participation in Being itself, a Being beyond all categories of thought. Man is to be saved through a Deity "at once the Monad, the Absolute, and the prime Cause, a God who was the source and sanction of ethical idealism, and the goal of his mystical aspiration." [29] Philo "found in his typology two definite things, the Road to the Greek Absolute, and a vindication of the unique truth of Judaism. In his exclusiveness he stands out as a Jew. But he is a man of the Hellenistic Age in his attempt to keep typology subordinate to metaphysics. It was for Christian theologians two centuries or more later to subordinate metaphysics to typology." [30]

VI. The Higher Law

How is it possible, the reader may ask, that Philo should find in the Torah something even remotely similar to the mystical approach that formed the climax of Greek thought? The reason is that for Philo the "Jewish law" is but an aspect of his entire philosophy of law. And this general philosophy of law is expressed in the Form-Matter scheme of the Greeks. Philo assumes that when in the Genesis narrative Moses speaks of creation he uses what is tantamount to this Greek scheme. Moses has his formless matter which God finds and upon which he impresses form.[31]

"In the De Opificio Philo makes a great deal of this conception that creation was the giving of form to formless matter, but even in that treatise creation in this sense is throughout subservient to the notion that creation was a process of imposing Law upon matter. To Philo the first chapters of Genesis have for their purpose the implication that the cosmos sings in harmony with the Law and the Law with the cosmos, and that the law-abiding man is forthwith

13

a citizen of the cosmos, for he is one who regulates his actions in accordance with the will of nature, that nature in accordance with which the whole cosmos is ruled." [32]

When the true covenant-keeping Jew obeyed the law of Moses he "obeyed, more basically, the law of nature." [33] "Nature's 'will' is the norm of the cosmos." Of course Philo wants no materialism, no monism, no pantheism. The ethical consciousness of man requires that God be above nature and that nature be subject to him. Philo therefore seeks for the primacy of the spiritual. He finds this in Moses and in Plato. "The Law of God, or the Law of Nature, may thus be considered independently of the anomalous natural law of matter." [34]

Here we come back to the Logos. For the law, the *Nomos*, is, for Philo, identical with the Logos, not in the monistic sense of Stoicism but in a way that makes *Nomos* both transcendent to and immanent in the universe.

VII. The Torah

With this general view of *Nomos* or Logos as both above and within the universe we return to a more detailed consideration of the law of Moses. And we shall not need to fear a reintroduction of obscurantism at this point. There will be no literalism and externalism in respect to the giving of the law or with respect to the law itself. Moses will give verbal expression to the law of God or law of nature as it is found in the ethical consciousness of every man.

But think not that Philo has forgotten the uniqueness of the law of Moses. Says Goodenough: "When one turns to Philo's notion of Jewish Law it is clear that Jewish apologetic fervor has been the inspiration of this intensified stress upon Law in general. By magnifying Law, and by orienting Jewish Law with Natural Law as the Law of God, the Jew could present his religion as the solution of the Greek problem, or of the mystic search of the Hellenistic Age.

"No more patent fact springs out of the pages of Philo than his loyalty to Judaism. He was loyal to the Jewish group in Alexandria, loyal to the race as a whole, but most of all loyal to the Jewish Law, and his treatment of the Law is so Jewish that his writings are frequently only intelligible when the Jewish attitude toward the Torah is kept in mind along with the Greek conception of nomos." [35]

How otherwise than by "orienting Jewish Law with Natural Law as the Law of God" could the Jew fulfill his world-wide mission? The Jewish *nomos* undoubtedly meant for Philo "the divine revelation of truth." [36] But there opened up to the vision of Philo deeper depths and higher heights of this Jewish law than to any Jew before him. Philo saw that he could find an *Anknüpfungspunkt* for the revelation of Moses in the ethical consciousness of mankind in general. And thus there would be a guarantee of acceptance for the gospel of salvation-by-the-works-of-the-law which the God of Israel in his "sovereign grace" and "providence" helped Israel to illustrate before the eyes of an astounded world.

The word *illustrate* is used advisedly. For Abraham, the father of the faithful, must be called such because he illustrates the Torah, the proper way of life." [37] It is the Pentateuch as a whole that "teaches Philo his Judaism." [38] "Philo revered the Torah on the ground that it was a revelation of the existence and nature of God, and of God's higher Law of Nature. In spite of his endless concern with details of the letter, he studied the Law for what he could make of it as a whole, rather than for its literal content. He could not logically have had this attitude to the whole without retaining respect for the letter as such." [39]

Did Philo then minimize the significance of individual laws? Not in the least. He greatly prized them. But he prized them as particularizations of the Torah as a whole and the Torah as a whole as a particularization of the Law of Nature.[40] The reader will observe how completely free this enthusiast for the law of Moses and for all its details has kept himself from all "obscurantism." The most detailed laws of Moses will readily be owned as proper and divine by the sensitive ethical consciousness of every spiritually minded Gentile. "Philo was a fastidious observer of the Law" as he lived among his Gentile neighbors.[41] But in doing so he virtually asks nothing more of these neighbors than to live up to the best ethical ideals that they find within them.

Does this liberal interpretation of the law of Moses set off Philo's view from that of "normative" Rabbinic Judaism? Goodenough thinks that it does. Says he: "Philo was a fastidious observer of the Law. Yet, except in the little address, *On Blessings and Curses,* his legalism was not the legalism of 'normative' Judaism. Apart from the controversy between Pharisees and Sadducees over the validity

15

of the oral tradition, all that we know of normative Jewish piety, especially as that piety was immortalized for all classes in the great Psalter, indicates a sense of the ultimate and inherent value of obedience to the Law quite in itself. The difference between Philo in his three great commentaries and this type of legalism lies in an ultimate divergence as to the meaning and content of virtue. The normative point of view developed inevitably into rabbinism, which had primarily the legalist's, not the philosopher's, approach to law and life. Many philosophers of significance have enriched the stream of Jewish tradition, but their speculations have not been in the main current. That main current has from the beginning been channeled by the Jewish assumption that virtue was a matter of exactly, and sincerely, fulfilling the commands of God, and the Jew has always been proud of the privilege of doing so. By Jews the Law has chiefly been treated as lawyers treat the law, with the written code as a precedent for application rather than as a principle of ethics in the philosopher's sense. The Jew got his reward in the assurance that God was pleased with him for his obedience, and would mercifully help him back into the path if he had faltered but wanted sincerely to be reinstated as an obedient child." [42]

We cannot believe that Goodenough's contrast between Philo and normative Judaism is true to the facts. As we shall see in a later chapter, normative or Rabbinic Judaism itself adopted the idea of the unwritten Torah. Now, apart from the debatable question as to the measure of Philo's acquaintance with the Rabbinic tradition, it is clear that the idea of the Unwritten Torah and Philo's idea of the Torah as the expression of the Law of Nature found in essence everywhere among men is basically the same. The foundation of both is the assumption that the ethical consciousness of man projects a god who, though utterly transcendent above man, yet makes his will known in the conscience of man.

To be sure, the Pharisees were in a sense legalists. But so is every one who finds the foundation of ethics in man's moral consciousness as such. To be sure, the Pharisees were arbitrary in their interpretation of the law, but so is every one who depends upon the autonomous moral consciousness as his ultimate standard of right and wrong.

16

VIII. *The Mystic Moses*

That Philo reduces the Old Testament revelation to virtual identity with the non-historical thought of Greek philosophy and the eastern mystery religions can be seen from his total reduction of the significance of Moses to that of the supreme illustration of the mystic way by which man can find absorption into nameless being.

Philo changes the Torah "into a great allegory." [43] "The Patriarchs, and especially Moses, are the great revelation of the higher Way. Sometimes Philo groups them to show that each reveals a different aspect of the struggle to rise, or of mystic achievement. But each Patriarch is really one who has achieved the end of the Mystery. The first triad of Patriarchs, for example, is Enos, Enoch, and Noah. Each of these represents a preliminary stage; Enos, Hope, Enoch, Repentance, and Noah, the achievement of *dikaiosune* by the destruction of the passions. These men may thus be treated as preliminary steps on the mystic ladder, or any one of them may be referred to as representing the ultimate experience. But Noah is emphasized much more than the other two since his being confined in the ark represented the soul shut up in the body with the passions through the time of purification, and his coming out of the ark the great experience of delivery from material bondage that he might rise to saintliness for himself and saving power for others.

"It is through Abraham, Isaac, and Jacob that the Mystery is first fully developed. Abraham and Jacob are treated from the point of view of ascent through the Powers to the Logos, though the Sophia-marriage theme is developed in connection with their marriages. Abraham goes out from Chaldea, as Jacob runs from Esau, to typify the first step, the running away from the life of dependence upon matter, from the life of unrestrained response to passions and perceptions, from the life of confused thinking in which matter is regarded as the ultimate. This step is also represented in the allegory of the migration of the Israelites by the departure from Egypt. The flight is only one step in the preliminary emancipation from matter; the second step is a definite renunciation of the somatic life, what Paul would call dying to the body but what Philo more correctly calls killing the body. This is the stage in the migration represented by the drowning of the Egyptians in the Red Sea. The

17

corresponding stage in the story of Abraham is lost, if it was included, through the fact that the section of the *Quæstiones* which might have given it is not preserved. But it may well have been omitted from the story of Abraham, for this step may be identified, according to the necessities of tracing spiritual progress through the recorded incidents in the lives of the Patriarchs, with either the flight from the body or the going up to the great final experience after the period of discipline." [44]

Moses tells us about the patriarchs. For him they are the incarnation of the Torah. Among them Abraham is of special interest. "When Abraham left materialistic pantheism he went to Charran, the land of senses, to begin at the bottom to observe the world for himself. But the senses are useless without the mind to interpret their perceptions. When Abraham's mind had thus been freed of false opinion, so that it could consider the world, he at once concluded that there must be a mind behind the visible universe as there is one behind the material aspects of a man. First, he got this as a conception, since he could not with his physical sight endure the contemplating of the divine Light-Rays. And yet his getting the right conception was followed by God's revealing Himself to Abraham, for the right conception had removed the veil that made such a vision impossible, though even then God had to take the initiative in revealing Himself to Abraham, since without special action of God no man can get the Vision." [45]

Abraham therefore "typifies the virtuous mind," the keeper of the Torah.[46] "Beginning with an apprehension of the existence of God as a true doctrine, Abraham went on to regiment his own nature so that the mind was completely dominant, and free to look up to God. He was met with two dispensations: he was solidified in his virtuous life by the immediate action of Virtue within him, the mystic marriage, and then he was able to go on to a mystic vision of God in His true nature. To God as He was now fully apprehended he dedicated his life completely, even to the abandoning of the quest for happiness, and was finally rewarded by being given happiness in God. Many more things could be said on the subject, says Philo, but this is adequate." [47]

We must omit Isaac and Jacob and go at once to Moses. Philo wants to convert the Gentile to a life according to the Torah. And Moses not only illustrates the mystic way but also sets it forth in

18

words. The Gentile must be led to him. Moses, as was Isaac, is "self-taught." "His life was characterized by a perfect harmony of thoughts, ideals, words and actions." [48] "Like the typical king, Moses was oriented in the Law of Nature, the orthos logos." [49] "When Moses by holding up his hands brought victory to the Israelites over Amalek he showed that the soul can triumph over mortal things only as the mind is borne aloft above them." [50] "Moses sitting outside the camp is really then a type of the perfect mystic who, having gone beyond the experience of the Logos in the Cosmos, comes to the higher doctrines of the Mystery, and can live simply and continuously on that level. Indeed he is that Logos itself." [51]

It is obvious that Moses, as thus presented, represents the mystic man. He represents the idea of "the mystery." In his *Allegory* Philo moves beyond specific commands into the realm of absorption into pure being.[52] This is not to say that for Philo specific commands are of no importance. We have seen the reverse to be true. But it does mean that for him, Judaism, so far from being identified with a detailed code of externally promulgated laws, stands primarily for the high ethical ideals of a generally spiritual absorption of man into Deity.

But if Philo sought to bring Gentiles into acceptance of the ideal of life so fully and perfectly represented by the Mystic Moses, did he ask them to accept anything that they did not already possess? We cannot think so. Everything that Philo finds in the Old Testament centers about the idea of Mystery. The allegorical handling of both the narrative and the legal material of the Torah is controlled by one idea, namely, that of the Mystic Moses. And with this idea, Mystery and the Mystic Moses, Philo had nothing new to offer to his Alexandian neighbors. Says Goodenough: "It is quite possible and probable, then, that for two centuries or more before Philo the Jews in Egypt, especially in Alexandria, found in their environment that type of thought ready made which we can only describe by an extended hyphenization, a Persian-Isiac-Platonic-Pythagorean mystery. This ready made blend was the nearest thing to Judaism in their environment, for it alone was a philosophy built upon the personal apprehension of an exalted and monotheistic Deity." [53]

IX. The Alexandrian Apologetic

Julius Guttman notes: "The affinity of Jewish monotheism with the concept of God as developed by the philosophers had been recognized by both sides at an early date." [54]

The Jews in Alexandria, says Guttman, "called their religion a philosophy, and in their apologetics sought to demonstrate the philosophic character of the Jewish idea of God and the humane nature of Jewish ethics. They laid the foundations for the attempt to provide a philosophical form for the intellectual content of Judaism, clothing it in Greek modes of expression and using philosophical arguments in support of the ethical doctrines of the Bible. Not only the form but the content of Greek philosophy also invaded Judaism. The manner and extent of this penetration varied, ranging from the mere philosophical embellishment of Jewish ideas, to their replacement by Greek doctrines, and culminating in the radical philosophical sublimation undertaken by Philo." [55]

It is this "radical philosophical sublimation" that is accomplished by means of allegorization. "For Philo, philosophy is not merely a convenient means for an exposition of his ideas, nor is the acceptance of philosophic doctrines limited to details only; Judaism as a whole is conceived as a philosophic doctrine inasmuch as it contains a complete system of philosophy. With the aid of the allegorical method evolved by the Stoics, Philo succeeded in preaching a philosophical reinterpretation of both the historical and the legal parts of the Pentateuch; he was sincerely convinced that he was not misrepresenting Judaism but revealing its deepest meaning. The extent to which he was rooted in Judaism is borne out by the literary form of his writings, most of which are commentaries on the Torah and probably originated from homilies delivered in the synagogue. The substance of his teaching also exhibits Jewish elements, though these appear in the sentiments underlying it rather than in its conceptional content. But on the whole, Philo's system can only be understood in terms of its Greek presuppositions.

"In the wake of Posidonius' synthesis of Platonic and Stoic doctrines, Philo reduces the whole of reality to two factors. The two ultimate principles in the world are the active divine cause and matter, which is the object of divine causality. The idea of a formless primal matter, which was mentioned in the Book of Wisdom only in passing, becomes one of the main pillars of Philo's system; the scriptural doctrine of creation gives way to the notion of the fashioning of the world out of formless matter. Of course, the relationship between God and the world is not seen in terms of Stoic pantheism. Philo's God is not the Greek *pneuma* that fills the world; he stands over and against the world in absolute transcendence, and unlike the Stoic *pneuma* is conceived as absolutely immaterial. Quite rightly, the influence of the traditional Jewish idea of God has been detected in the Philonic emphasis on God's transcendence and spirituality. However, the effect of this influence seems to manifest itself more in Philo's rejection of Stoic materialism and pantheism than in the concept of a personal God, which, in fact, is completely missing.

"Philo's sublimation of the concept of God is not fulfilled merely by ridding it of all anthopomorphic characteristics; actually the concept of God is elevated above all values and perfections conceivable to the human mind. God is above knowledge and virtue, above the good and the beautiful. Since God is exalted above all that is knowable, only his bare existence is accessible to our intellect; in fact, Philo prefers to describe God as 'He Who Is,' or in even more abstract language, as 'Being.' The direction in which Philo developed the concept of God had already been anticipated by Plato. But Philo went far beyond Plato, and for the first time gave to the notion of divine transcendence the radical twist of later negative theology. If God is also described as the sum of all perfection, this is but the reverse side of the same idea, and though this also seems to open the door again to the habit of predicating personal attributes to God—calling him Father and Creator, or speaking of his grace and goodness—this result was certainly not seriously intended by Philo. Consistency was never Philo's strong point; if he occasionally seems to approach the biblical conception of a personal God, this may more safely be considered inconsistency rather than the essential nature of his teaching." [56]

With this summary by Guttman, we must leave Philo.

The Jews were conscious of their mission as teachers of all mankind in the revelation of the only true God to Moses. In Alexandria, and at the beginning of the common era, Philo undertakes to give a fuller and more self-articulated statement of this world mission than any Jew before him had given. But since he does not read the Old Testament in terms of its fulfillment in Christ, he must needs demythologize it and thereby reduce its message to that which the higher religions of the East and the best philosophy of the Greeks already knew. Henceforth, the Gentile and the Jews are both alike in their hopeless attachment to a meaningless philosophy and an ethic of despair.

NOTES

1. James Drummond, *Philo Judæus; or The Jewish-Alexandrian Philosophy in its Development and Completion* (London: Williams and Norgate, 1888), I, 1.
2. *Ibid.*, II, 273.
3. *Ibid.*
4. *Ibid.*
5. *Ibid.*
6. Harry Austryn Wolfson, *Philo* (Cambridge, Mass.: Harvard University Press, 1947), I, 200.
7. *Ibid.*
8. *Ibid.*, p. 217.
9. Wolfson, *Philo,* II, 74.
10. *Ibid.*, p. 75.
11. *Ibid.*, pp. 75-76.
12. Cf. Wolfson, *op. cit.*, II, 111.
13. *Ibid.*
14. *Ibid.*
15. *Ibid.*, p. 113.
16. *Ibid.*, p. 115.
17. *Ibid.*
18. *Ibid.*, p. 116.
19. *Ibid.*
20. *Ibid.*, pp. 119-120.
21. Drummond, *op. cit.*, I, 323.
22. *Ibid.*, p. 324.
23. *Ibid.*, p.. 325.
24. Cf. Drummond, *op. cit.*, II, 11.
25. Wolfson, *op. cit.*, I, 253.
26. Edwin R. Goodenough, *By Light, Light* (New Haven: Yale University Press, 1935).
27. *Ibid.*, p. 11.
28. *Ibid.*
29. *Ibid.*, p. 46.
30. *Ibid.*, p. 47.

31. *Ibid.*, pp. 48-49.
32. *Ibid.*, p. 49.
33. *Ibid.*
34. *Ibid.*, p. 54.
35. *Ibid.*, p. 72.
36. *Ibid.*, p. 73.
37. *Ibid.*, p. 74.
38. *Ibid.*, p. 80.
39. *Ibid.*
40. *Ibid.*
41. *Ibid.*, p. 84.
42. *Ibid.*, pp. 84-85.
43. *Ibid.*, p. 235.
44. *Ibid.*, p. 238.
45. *Ibid.*, p. 138.
46. *Ibid.*, p. 139.
47. *Ibid.*, p. 142.
48. *Ibid.*, p. 183.
49. *Ibid.*, p. 184.
50. *Ibid.*, p. 211.
51. *Ibid.*
52. *Ibid.*, p. 215.
53. *Ibid.*, p. 237.
54. Julius Guttman, *Philosophies of Judaism* (New York: Holt, Rinehart and Winston, 1964), p. 21.
55. *Ibid.*
56. *Ibid.*, pp. 24-25.

CHAPTER II

TWO TYPES OF FAITH

Shortly before Immanuel came into the world it was foretold of him that he came to save his people from their sin. In its most comprehensive sense the mission of Jesus as the Christ may be expressed in the words of John 3:16: "For God so loved the world, that he gave his only begotten Son, that whosoever believeth in him should not perish, but have everlasting life."

This comprehensive statement includes the Jews as a nation. But just as the saving of the world does not imply the saving of every man living in the world, so the saving of the Jewish nation does not imply the saving of every Jew. Because of sin, all men, Jew and Gentile alike, are in the way of death. Only those who believe in Jesus Christ as their Savior from sin are saved from the wrath to come. All men fell in Adam (Rom. 5:12). Through Adam's sin all men became covenant-breakers. The covenant is God's dialogue with man. In this dialogue God is original and man is derivative, dependent, and subordinate. But through sin man sought to be original and to make God derivative, dependent, and subordinate.

Of course, man was not able actually to reduce God to a derivative position. And, of course, man was not able to escape the frustration involved in thinking of himself as being original. All of the efforts of sinful man to interpret himself and his world in terms of himself as sulf-sufficient, and therefore as absolutely free, indicate internal confusion.

Even the "highest" and "noblest" efforts of sinful men exhibit the futility of every attempt to find meaning in life apart from the fear of the Lord which is the *beginning* of wisdom. In fact, it is

25

the "highest" and "noblest" efforts of the would-be autonomous or natural man which exhibit this futility in most striking form. There are among these "highest" and "noblest" of philosophies of life those that *make room* for Jesus Christ. But so long as men do not accede to Jesus Christ the place that is his rightly, namely, Son of God, one with the Father, saving men from the wrath of God deservedly resting upon them, by the sacrifice of himself on the cross, so long will men continue under this wrath.

All men are confronted with God's speech in the world. Every fact of the world embodies the covenantal requirement of the Creator to man his creature. But man seeks to repress the knowledge of God within him (Rom. 1:18). Men are also confronted with the Christ who came into the world. "He was in the world, and the world was made by him and the world knew him not. He came unto his own, and his own received him not. But as many as received him, to them gave he power to become the sons of God, even to them that believe on his name: which were born not of blood, nor of the will of the flesh, nor of the will of man, but of God" (Jn. 1:10-13).

It thus appears that the Jews, *together with all men,* (a) know God and (b) seek to suppress this knowledge of God. God in Christ speaks to all men, including the Jews. But all men, again including the Jews, answer by seeking to escape from the voice of God. All men are prodigals who know that they have left the Father's house. All men, as it were, hear the Father's voice pursuing them as they are on their way to the swine trough. The goodness of God to all men, even to all sinful men, is calculated to lead them to repentance (Rom. 2:2).

But if the Jews resemble men in general in that (a) they know God and (b) they seek to escape the voice of God, there is yet a special sense in which God in Christ deals with the Jews. Through Abraham and his seed the nations were to be blessed. Christ preached first of all to the lost sheep of the house of Israel. He wept over Jerusalem, desiring that he might gather its children as a hen gathers her chicks under her wings. He grieved over the Jews' rejection of him. And Paul has "great heaviness and continual sorrow" in his heart because his kinsmen according to the flesh persist in the sort of rejection of Christ of which, before his conversion, he himself had been guilty. They are, he says, Israelites,

26

the giving of the law, and the service of God, and the promises pertain to them. The climax of it all Paul expresses when he says: "Whose are the fathers, and of whom as concerning the flesh Christ came, who is over all, God blessed for ever, Amen" (Rom. 9:2-5).

God in Christ seeks all men, including the Jew. There is great joy in heaven when one Jew repents.

I. Buber and New Testament Faith

With this background in mind we turn to Martin Buber. Here is a modern Jew steeped both in Jewish lore and in modern philosophy. Here is a Jew who informs us that for nearly fifty years the New Testament has been "a main concern" in his studies.[1] Says Buber: "From my youth onwards I have found in Jesus my great brother. That Christianity has regarded and does regard him as God and Saviour has always appeared to me a fact of highest importance which, for his sake and my own, I must endeavor to understand. A small part of the results of this desire to understand is recorded here. My own fraternally open relationship to him has grown ever stronger and clearer, and today I see him more strongly and clearly than ever before. I am more than ever certain that a great place belongs to him in Israel's history of faith and that this place cannot be described by any of the usual categories." [2]
and as such the adoption, and the glory, and the covenants, and

In the teaching of Jesus, "as we know it from the early texts of the gospels," says Buber, "the genuinely Jewish principle is manifest." [3] The Protestant may find it hard to believe his eyes when he reads "It becomes evident that Jesus and central Pharisaism belong essentially together. . . ." [4]

How different this attitude of Buber's seems to be from that of Caiaphas, the high priest, who tore his clothes saying: "He hath spoken blasphemy," when Jesus claimed to be the Son of God and Son of Man (Mt. 26:65).

Have not the Jews throughout the ages regarded themselves as the guardians of monotheism? Have not Christians, because of their belief in Christ as the Son of God and in the Holy Spirit, been regarded by the Jews as idolaters? Has Buber virtually repudiated the true Jewish principle when he says that Jesus shares it with him?

We can answer these questions in some measure if we inquire into what Buber thinks the nature of the Faith to be.

27

The title of our present chapter is taken from that of a book by Buber. "There are," says Buber, "and can be in the end only two types of faith." [5] Both of these kinds of faith, he adds, "can be understood from the simple data of our life: the one from the fact that I trust someone, without being able to offer sufficient reasons for my trust in him; the other from the fact that, likewise without being able to give a sufficient reason, I acknowledge a thing to be true." [6] We may in general, says Buber, speak of the former as Jewish and of the second as Christian. But the distinction is not absolute. For in early Christianity the Christian type of faith was joined with the Jewish one.[7]

Gradually the two types of faith appear to be in contrast with one another. The "Jesus of the genuine tradition" still shares the Jewish faith, the faith of trust. But "the Jesus of theology" belongs to a different kind of faith.[8]

The nature of this different faith springs from Greece. To be sure, when the writer of Hebrews defines faith as the "assurance of what is hoped for" he still uses the idea of faith as trust. But when faith is said to involve a "conviction of things unseen" then we are in the realm of intellectual demonstration. "He who has faith in the sense of the Epistle to the Hebrews has received proof of the existence of that, the existence of which admits of no observation." [9] This sort of faith is no longer the faith of the "true Israelite." The true Israelite "trusts in the God Who exists 'as a matter of course' as truly his God." [10] The true Israelite "does not need to be convinced of what he does not see: what he sees he sees in the faith of the invisible." [11]

It is "that gigantic figure, Paul, whom we must regard as the originator of the Christian conception of faith. . . ." [12]

But how then, asks Buber, can one account for the fact that Paul appeals to Abraham as the father of those who truly have faith (Rom. iv)? Buber replies that it is said of Abraham in Genesis that he "continued to trust" God and it is said of God "that He 'deemed' this 'as the proving true' of him." [13] "What is recorded of Abraham is an immovable steadfastness. . . ." [14] And God, who knows the heart of man, "can deem anything which happens in a man and which proceeds from him as the full realization of the essential relationship to the Godhead. For in this moment, in this movement of his total being, the person has raised himself to that

28

position which is decisive for the revelation of his worth; the nature of the creature has attained the being intended by the creation, and even the most extreme 'temptation' will only be able to draw forth and realize what was then ordained." [15]

But "Paul found in his Greek Bible at this point something which is immersed in a different atmosphere. Abraham does not believe 'in' God, in the sense of perseverance in Him, but he believes Him. . . ." [16] And then, in addition, Paul substitutes for the "divine consideration, deeming, ratification" the idea of a "category in the judicial computation of items of guilt and innocence against each other, and in connexion with this instead of the proving true, a 'righteousness,' the rightness of the conduct which justifies the individual before God; both are a limitation, a deflation of that original fulness of life, a limitation common to Alexandrian and contemporary rabbinical Judaism." [17]

Thus Paul changes the import of the faith of Abraham. "The simple face-to-face relationship between God and man in the Genesis story is replaced by an interpenetration which comes about by faith and faith alone, the dialogical by the mystical situation." [18]

We are now "removed on to a rocky slope where the inner divine dialectic governs exclusively." [19]

It is of basic importance for us to understand what Buber intends us to understand by the "inner divine dialectic" which he ascribes to Paul's conception of faith. We quote Buber fully on this point: "The fundamentals of this dialectic-idea are to be found in Judaism, namely in the early Talmud, but the conception of the intercourse between the divine attributes of severity and of mercy changes here to the extreme real paradox, by which for Paul (here we are obliged to anticipate for a moment the course of this investigation) even the great theme of his faith, his Christology, is supported, without it being possible to be expressed: in redeeming the world by the surrender of His son God redeems Himself from the fate of His justice, which would condemn it." [20]

It appears then that for Buber the Pauline view of the nature of faith and the Pauline view of the object of faith imply one another. Furthermore, Buber already at this early point indicates his basic objection to the total Christian scheme of God and his relation to man. The God of Paul's theology finds himself in a predicament. There is first "the fate of His justice" which would condemn the

29

world, and in condemning the world God would himself be the victim of this fate. He therefore surrenders his Son in order to redeem himself from this fate.

Buber goes on at once to point out that Paul's entire teaching of justification by faith rather than by works grows out of this view of the ultra-divine dialectic. How else can we understand what Paul means when he says: "He therefore that ministereth to you the Spirit, and worketh miracles among you, doeth he it by the works of the law, or by the hearing of faith? Even as Abraham believed God and it was accounted to him for righteousness. Know ye therefore that they which are of faith, the same are the children of Abraham" (Gal. 3:5-7).

Here, says Buber, the transformation of Israel's conception of faith becomes very clear. Paul was evidently thinking of Leviticus 18:5 where "God decrees that His statutes and commandments should be kept, in which and through which the man who does them lives." [21] And now Paul substitutes the life of faith for that which derives from doing. "In the place of the life derived from doing has come the life from faith; from this alone there comes and into this alone there enters now 'the righteousness of God,' His declaration of man as righteous:" [22]

But how, asks Buber, could Abraham have held to such a faith as Paul describes? "The faith which Paul indicates in his distinction between it and the law is not one which could have been held in the pre-Christian era." [23] The righteousness of God of which Paul speaks "is that which is through faith in Christ (Rom. 3:22, Gal. 2:16), which means faith in one who has come, died on the cross and risen." [24]

When Paul refers to Isaiah 8:14 which speaks of "a stone of stumbling" and of a "rock of offense," this cannot refer to "ancient Israel and a possible insufficiency of its faith in the future coming of the Messiah, but only to the Jews of that time, those whom Paul sought for Christ and whom he had not won for him because they did not recognize in him the promised Messiah of belief." [25] And herewith Paul's claim that Christ is the end of the law, so that righteousness may come to everyone that believes "falls to the ground." [26]

Of the whole Pauline discussion of faith as opposed to the work of the law it must be said that not only the "Old Testament belief and the living faith of post-Biblical Judaism" are opposed to it "but also the Jesus of the Sermon on the Mount. . . ." [27]

There is, of course, a difference between what the Pharisees teach and what Jesus teaches. But on the basic matter of inwardness they are agreed. "The Scripture-verse (Deut. 6:6), 'This, which I this day command thee, shall be on they heart' is explained (Bab. Megilla 20a) to mean that everything depends on the direction of the heart." [28] The famous adage, "A scholar whose inwardness does not equal his outwardness is no scholar," confirms this emphasis upon the fact that mere outward compliance with the letter of the law is not enough. "In the Hebrew Bible Torah does not mean law, but direction, instruction, information. *Moreh* means not law-giver but teacher." [29]

To be sure, the true idea of the Torah tended to be taken as a static book of laws.[30] The idea "that Israel possesses it tends effectively to supplant the vital contact with the ever-living revelation and instruction, a contact which springs from the depth of the primitive faith. But the actuality of faith, the undying strength of hearing the Word, was strong enough to prevent torpidity and to liberate again and again the living idea. This inner dialectic of Having and Being is in fact the main moving force in the spiritual hstory of Israel." [31]

In all this, says Buber, the Jesus of the Sermon on the Mount agrees with the true Judaistic concept of faith.

There is, even so, a point of difference between Jesus and the Pharisees. When Jesus said "Ye therefore shall be perfect," he was using an essentially eschatological approach. The Old Testament command, "Ye shall be holy, for I am holy," is not eschatological. There "is no perfection in the course of history." What the Torah wants men to strive for is "completeness, undividedness, entirety, in the relation to God." The Torah addresses the constant nature of man and summons him to the elevation granted to him, to the highest realization of his relationship to God which is possible to him as a mortal being; Jesus on the other hand, as represented by Matthew, means to summon the elect in the castastrophe of humanity to come as near to God as is made possible to it only in the catas-trophe." [32]

Now the Pharisees carried forth the idea of the Torah. Their teaching is that the heart of man "is by nature without direction. . . .;

31

only in Emunah is persistence: there is not true direction except to God. But the heart cannot receive this direction from the human spirit, but only from a life lived in the will of God. Hence the Torah has assigned to man actions agreeable to God, in the doing of which he learns to direct his heart to Him. According to this purpose of the Torah the decisive significance and value does not lie in the bulk of these actions in themselves but in the direction of the heart in them and through them." [33]

It appears then that "Jesus, as he speaks in the Sermon on the Mount, considers the Torah capable of fulfilment. . . ." [34] In contradiction to this position of the Jews and Jesus, Paul argues that the Torah is incapable of fulfilment. [35] But even more basic than this is the fact that according to Paul the Torah was given "not in order to be fulfilled but rather through its incapability of fulfillment to call forth sin . . . and so prepare the way for grace." [36] Thus it appears that according to Paul "one aim of the divine Lawgiver" is "to make His own law ineffectual." [37]

Here we are back to what Buber earlier spoke of as the "inner divine dialectic." [38] On Paul's view, Buber contends, God must not only redeem himself from his own fate but also assigns his creatures to unavoidable self-frustration in their use of his law. Paul himself trembles as he speaks of "the mystery predetermined by God" pertaining particularly to those "who were assigned the principal roles in it, namely the spirits which Paul calls the rulers of this aeon and whose leader he calls on occasion (2 Cor. 4:4) the god of this aeon. For if they had known it 'they would not have crucified the Lord of Glory' (1 Cor. 2:8), but this was destined for them in the mystery so that thereby they help to achieve its realization and to promote their own overthrow." [39]

It is obvious, argues Buber, that having such a conception of God and of man we may expect Paul to hold to an equally confusing and reprehensible view of salvation. Here too we may expect to find determinism of a dreadful nature.

According to Paul God hardens whom he will. On his view sin "is not an undertaking which man can break off when the situation becomes critical, but a process started by him, the control of which is withdrawn from him at a fixed moment." [40] Remember Pharoah! Contrary to Old Testament teaching with respect to the "hardening" of men's hearts, Paul's usage of this term "no longer cares about

32

the men and the generations of men which it affects, but uses them and uses them up for higher ends. Contrary to the Old Testament, Paul's God does not have regard for the people to whom He speaks out of the cloud, or rather causes His angels to speak." [41] The God of Paul "has actually 'shut them all in unbelief', the Gentiles without the law and the Jews who possess it, 'so that He might have mercy upon all.' " [42]

Buber's reaction to all this is well expressed when he says: "When I contemplate this God I no longer recognize the God of Jesus nor his world in this world of Paul's." [43] Jesus "was concerned with the individual human soul and with every human soul. . . ." [44] For him it was true of every soul which had lived from Moses to himself belonging to Israel, that "when they had gone astray, turning was allowed, and everyone of them, when they did turn back, was the lost son returned home." [45]

"In Paul's conception of God, where the generations of souls in Israel from Moses to Jesus are concerned, this characteristic is supplanted by another, which alters everything. I do not venture to give it a name." [46]

II. Buber and Modern Philosophy

Up to this point we have dealt mainly with Buber's evaluation of Jesus on the basis of Scripture exegesis. We turn now to a consideration of his place in modern philosophy. This will help us, to some extent at least, to ascertain the basic principles which he employs in his exegesis. And this will, in turn, help us to understand his reason for thinking that he can put Jesus into the class who follow the Jewish principle but who must oppose Paul in his basic contentions.

The truth or untruth of Judaism cannot be settled, thinks Buber, simply by exegesis. Ultimately it is a question of the nature of reality. When he discusses a question like that of the resurrection of Jesus he says simply: "We can only realize anew that the resurrection of an individual person does not belong to the realm of ideas of the Jewish world." [47] When Thomas, confronted by Jesus, called him his Lord and his God, he therewith forsook the world of Jewish thought. For with his confession "the presence of the One Who cannot be represented, the paradox of Emunah, is replaced by the binitarian image of God, one aspect of which, turned toward the man, shows him a human face." [48]

Recognizing Jesus as God, as Thomas did, and as the gospel of John does, destroys the very principle of immediacy towards the imperceptible Being "which is God, that marks Israel's Emunah." [49]

Where then are we to find this principle of immediacy expressed? Of course, as the whole preceding discussion has shown, this principle is found in all the literature contained in the Talmud and in various Jewish writings. In particular it is found in the Hasidic movement. To this we shall return. For the moment we want to see how, according to Buber, it is also expressed in modern existential philosophy. In modern existentialism, Buber finds support for the Jewish type of faith. Moreover, the Jewish faith, when expressed philosophically, finds that it can lead modern existentialism toward a better expression of its faith than it has so far obtained. We refer to the I-Thou philosophy which Buber has himself developed. In it the principle of immediacy is expressed without danger of its falling into pantheism or mysticism.

It will be our concern to see how well Buber succeeds in escaping either of these or some other form of monologue philosophy after he rejects the covenantal dialogical thinking of Paul.

As is well known, in Buber's earliest philosophy he was sympathetic to mysticism, but in his latest philosophy he rejects mysticism in the interest of his I-Thou conception of the relation of God to man and man to God.

In 1923 Buber published his now famous book *I and Thou*. Then, in 1947, he published *Between Man and Man*. The first section of this second book has for its title "Dialogue" (Zwiesprache, 1929). Of this section he says: "The first of these works, *Dialogue* (1929), proceeded from the desire to clarify the 'dialogical' principle presented in *I and Thou*, to illustrate it and to make precise its relation to essential spheres of life." [50]

It is in terms of this dialogical principle, Buber argues, that the Jews know Jesus "from within." They know him "in the impulses and stirrings of his Jewish being, in a way that remains inaccessible to the peoples submissive to him." [51]

The far-reaching significance of this claim by Buber is expressed when he tells us of the remainder of a conversation during which he made this claim. His Christian friend and he stood up, "looked into the heart of one another's eyes" and "before everyone we gave one another the kiss of brotherhood." [52]

Thus "the discussion of the situation between Jews and Christians had been transformed into a bond between the Christian and the Jew. In this transformation dialogue was fulfilled. Opinions were gone, in a bodily way the factual took place." [53]

The frank statement here made by Buber expresses sharply the main arguments he carries on in several of his writings. When Buber says that he thinks of Jesus as his great brother, this is true only if Jesus is not his Savior and Lord. And when he gives his Christian friend the "kiss of brotherhood" he does this only if his Christian friend too will give up calling Jesus his Savior and Lord. When Buber says that not the Christian who sets up Christ as his absolute king but the Jew who denies him to be such knows him "from within," he is explaining Christ in terms of a principle that is above Christ.

In this basic respect Buber's attitude toward Christ is the same as that of the Pharisees. In saying this we are definitely not thinking of the question of open, personal animosity. We are thinking only of the basic principle by which one interprets life and reality as a whole. On this point Buber, no less than the Pharisees before him, has a view of God and his kingdom on earth, and of man and his origin and destiny, that assigns to Christ the same sort of place that is assigned to every other man. In Buber's scheme of things Christ is not the Son of God; he is not the Savior of sinners.

If Buber represents the position of modern Jews fairly, then we must think of Christ as weeping over them even as he did over Jerusalem and her children for their refusal to repent so that he might save them from their disobedience and hatred of him.

Hatred of Christ as the Son of God is tantamount to hatred of God as the Father.[53a] That is to say, he who is not a believer in Jesus Christ as the Son of God is not a believer in God. *He who is not a Christian is not, properly speaking, a theist.* Moreover, he who does not know Christ as the Son of God does not know him inwardly, i.e., for what he is. This means too that he does not know himself inwardly, i.e., for what he himself is. He who does not acknowledge Christ as his King, does not know himself as a creature of God and as a sinner before God. He does not know reality for what it is.

In particular, and this is the point of basic importance with respect to Buber, he does not know the nature of the dialogue between God and man. In consequence, he does not know the nature of dialogue between man and man.

The true nature of the dialogue between God and man can be understood only by those who know God through Jesus Christ his Son, who came to earth to redeem men. *True dialogue is man's covenantal interaction with the God of Scripture.*

Those who believe in Christ as the Son of God should therefore do precisely what Buber is doing. They must put their covenantal scheme over against that of Buber. Both schemes are all comprehensive. Buber holds that only on his I-Thou scheme can one find meaning in life at any point. Believers in Christ should claim that only on the *Christian I-Thou scheme* is it possible to find meaning in anything that confronts man.

The task of the Christian in relation to Buber is to show him that for all his claim to have a "dialogical" principle he is still engaged in *monologue*. He may reject the vulgar statement, *Glory to man in the highest,* but he does not escape the idea of pure human autonomy that underlies it.

One cannot find signs of God's address to man anywhere unless one finds them everywhere and unless one finds them as controlling the whole of history from its very beginning. This means that between Buber and the Christian the Old Testament as well as the New is in dispute. It is not as though Buber and the Christian both accept the Old Testament but that the Christian differs from Buber in that he accepts the New as well as the Old, while Buber accepts only the latter.

Christ told the Jews of his day that Moses and the Prophets spoke of him. Those who claimed to be expert in Moses and the Prophets, but who could not see the Old Testament Scriptures as, with one accord, pointing to Christ as the promised Messiah, were not experts at all. They might claim to be defenders of monotheism. So long as they said that Christ blasphemed when he called himself the Son of God they were not defenders of true monotheism at all. Moses and the Prophets are the servants of Christ, sent forth by him in order to have dialogue with men about him. He who does not see that Christ came to fulfill the law of Moses has not understood either Moses or the law. They who say that the Torah is the

36

great teacher of men but who do not see the Torah itself in the light of Christ as the Way, the Truth, and the Life have themselves, and not God, for their teacher.

All of these matters will need to be taken up for fuller discussion later. For the moment it must suffice to show that by enveloping Christ in his dialogical principle, Buber cannot escape falling into monologue.

Spinoza and Hasidism

Buber finds it necessary to set off his position from several movements of thought, past and present. He has been especially concerned with setting off his thought against that of Spinoza.

For Buber "God is the Eternal Thou whom man meets in the true 'life of dialogue.'" [54] Through his little book *I and Thou*, says Will Herberg, Buber proved himself to be a "pioneer" in the interest of a true personalist philosophy. Says Herberg further: "The self becomes a person, Buber taught, only in genuine personal relation to other selves. ('Through the Thou, a man becomes an I'); the person in community is the primal reality, and all authentic being emerges in the fulness of personal relation ('All real living is meeting'). It is as a personal relation that the divine-human encounter of faith is to be understood." [55] "Buber's man is dialogical man, the man 'who commits his whole being in God's dialogue with the world and who stands firm throughout this dialogue.' It is a dialogue in which 'God speaks to every man through the life which he gives him again and again . . . [and in which] man can only answer God with the whole of life, with the way in which he lives his given life.' This wholeness of response in the dialogue is the 'good' of man." [56]

Now, as we think of Spinoza, we think at the same time of another "remarkable Jew," namely, Sabbatai Zvi. "These two men mark a late exilic catastrophe of Judaism." Spinoza was excommunicated from the synagogue; Sabbatai Zvi was converted to Islam. Both "conducted to its conclusion a process which had begun with a single historical manifestation with Jesus." [57] As Sabbatai Zvi placed in question Jewish Messianism so Spinoza placed in question "the Jewish belief in God." [58]

Spinoza denied the reality of the great accomplishment of Israel. "The great deed of Israel is not that it taught the one real God, who

37

is the origin and goal of all being, but that it pointed out that this God can be addressed by man in reality, that man can say Thou to Him, that he can stand face to face with Him, that he can have intercourse with Him. Only Israel has understood, or rather actually lives, life as being addressed and answering, addressing and receiving answer." [59] For Israel "God is the God who can be addressed because He is the God who addresses." [60]

Now Christians allow God to be addressed only in conjunction with Christ." [61] We have seen earlier that these two positions are, for Buber, mutually exclusive.

Spinoza did not choose sides between these two positions. Certainly in leaving the Jewish principle he did not accept Christianity. It was rather Spinoza's purpose to purify God "from the stain of being open to address." [62] And "it is of great significance that only a Jew could teach men how to do away with it, and a Jew has done so." [63] Spinoza helped the mind of the intellectual among the peoples to liberate itself from that which had penetrated it; the tendency of the Western spirit toward monological life was decisively forwarded by him—and thereby the crisis of the spirit in general since in the air of monological life it must gloriously wither." [64]

Now how can we recover the true idea of Israel, the idea that God truly addresses man? Buber says that he found a basic reply to Spinoza in the position of Baal-Shem-Tov, leader of Hasidism.

Hasidism expresses the old idea of Israel anew and afresh. "Hasidism preserves undiminished God's distance from and superiority to the world in which He nonetheless dwells. In this distance Hasidism sets the undivided wholeness of human life in its full meaning: that it should receive the world from God and act on the world for the sake of God. Bound to the world, receiving and acting, man stands directly before God—not 'man' rather, but this particular man, you, I." [65]

In short, Hasidism thinks of the universe in which it lives sacramentally. Thinking of the world sacramentally leads to or implies thinking of it redemptively. "What we call 'evil' is not merely in man; it is in the world as the bad; it is the uncleanness of creation. But this uncleanness is not a nature, not an existent property of things. It is only its not standing firm, not finding direction, not deciding." [66]

38

The Hasidic view of evil, says Buber, is not gnostic. Hasidism has no sympathy for an ultimate dualism between good and evil. The origin of evil is through "a deed of the first man" inspired by the "serpent." "Now the incomplete cleaves to the completed creation; a suffering world, a world in need of God's redemption lies at God's feet. But He does not leave it to lie in the abyss of its strugglings; after the sparks of His creative fire fall into the things, His glory itself descends to the world, enters into it, into 'exile,' dwells in it, dwells with the troubled, the suffering creatures in the midst of their uncleanness—desiring to redeem them." [67]

It is obvious then that it is the idea of freedom, "freedom" in man and "freedom" in things, the "primal vessels," that can find no place in Spinoza's system. The "whole fulness of grace" is granted to the first men; "even the tree of life is not forbidden to them; . . . only just the mystery of the primal lack, the mystery of 'good and evil' God has reserved for Himself. But they did not stand firm before the fullness; they followed the promptings of the element of limitation. It is not as if they revolted against God; they do not decide against Him, only they just do not decide for Him. It is no rebellious movement; it is a perplexed, directionless, 'weak-minded,' indolent movement, this 'stretching out of the hand.' They do not do it, they have done it. One sees in them the directionless storming and plunging of the sparks in need of redemption—temptation, turmoil, and undecided deed. And so they 'know' the limited, of course, just as man, as men know, as Adam later 'knew' his wife; they know the limited, mixing themselves with it, knowing 'good-and-evil,' taking this good-and-evil into themselves, like plucked and eaten fruit." [68]

But redemption comes. "Man is the creature in whom the path of the world is concentrated and represented. As of himself he completes the fall, so he must be able of himself really to work on redemption. Does that mean that God is not able to redeem His world without man's cooperation? It means that God wills not to be able. Does God need man for His work? He wills to need him. God wills to need man for the work of completing His creation; in this sentence is to be grasped the foundation of the Jewish doctrine of redemption. But that God wills this means that this 'needing' becomes working reality; in history as it takes place, God waits for man." [69]

In this view of Hasidism, according to Buber, we have reinstated the dialogical principle over against the Spinozistic monologue. We have, at the same time, taken great care not to fall into the false dialogicism that centers around the idea of Jesus Christ as the Son of God. We have preserved the idea of God as ultimate mystery so flagrantly violated in the Christian concept of the finished revelation of God in Christ and in the words of his Apostles. Our faith holds that God "suffers with the fate of His world. And it is not merely in appearance that He waits for the initial movement toward redemption to come from the world—really initiating and not merely in appearance. How it happens that this is not appearance but reality, how something from out of His world, whether it be falling away or returning, can happen to God, the All-powerful and the All-knowing, that is a mystery of God the Creator and Redeemer, not more mysterious to me than that He is; and that He is to me almost less mysterious than that I am, I who write this with trembling fingers on a rock bench above a lake." [70]

Still further we have also found the "reply to that catastrophe of Jewish Messianism that stands under the name of Sabbatai Zvi." [71] Redemption takes place, not dramatically, but through the "servants of the Lord" who suffer in and for the world. Whatever, therefore, Jesus means to others, "seen from the standpoint of Judaism he is the first in the series of men who, stepping out of the hiddenness of the servant of the Lord, the real 'messianic mystery,' acknowledge their Messiahship in their souls and in their words. That this first one in the series was incomparably the purest, the most legitimate, the most endowed with real Messianic power—as I experience ever again when those personal words that ring true to me merge for me into a unity whose speaker becomes visible to me—alters nothing in the fact of this firstness; indeed it undoubtedly belongs just to it, to the fearfully penetrating reality that has characterized the whole automessianic series." [72]

Thus "the Hasidic message of redemption stands in opposition to the Messianic self-differentiation of one man from other men, of one time from other times, of one act from other actions. All mankind is accorded the co-working power, all time is directly redemptive, all action for the sake of God may be Messianic action. But only unpremeditated action can be action for the sake of God. The self-differentiation, the reflexion of man to a Messianic supe-

40

riority of this person, of this hour, of this action, destroys the unpremeditated quality of the act. Turning the whole of his life in the world to God and then allowing it to open and unfold in all its moments until the last—that is man's work toward redemption." [73]

Eclipse of God

In his *Eclipse of God* [74] Buber also speaks of Spinoza. In his doctrine of the divine attributes Spinoza seems to have undertaken "the greatest anti-anthropomorphic effort ever essayed by the human spirit." [75] But no such anti-anthropomorphic effort can possibly succeed. It leads to pure abstraction and to pure intellectualism. Spinoza himself was compelled to speak of the love of God.

We therefore look at "an argument against Spinoza" formulated by Immanuel Kant. To solve the relation between the idea of God as unconditioned or absolute who is nonetheless in relation to what is conditional he introduced his distinction between the pure and the practical reason. Giving up the idea of seeking for God with theoretical reason, Kant postulates him as "the source of all moral obligation." [76]

But even Kant did not clearly provide us with the I-Thou relation that we need when we speak of God. [77] And certainly Hegel did not. "The radical abstraction, with which philosophizing begins for Hegel, "ignores the existential reality of the I and of the Thou, together with that of everything else. According to Hegel, the absolute—universal reason the Idea, i.e., 'God'—uses everything that exists and develops in nature and in history, including everything that relates to man, as an instrument of its, i.e., God's, self-realization and perfect self-awareness; but God never enters into a living, direct relation to us, nor does He vouchsafe us such a relation to Him." [78]

We find in Hegel no "concrete *encounter*" between God and man. [79] In Hegel's thought, as he himself says, "individuals are sacrificed and surrendered." [80] In Hegel's view "God can no longer be for man that God which he encounters, both deeply mysterious and manifest, in his despairs and in his raptures." [81]

Turning next to Bergson, Buber says, we find that for him even more clearly than for Hegel, God is all process. And "to confine God to a producing function is to remove Him from the world in

41

which we live—a world filled with burning contradiction, and with yearning for salvation." [82]

On the other hand, continues Buber, "the conception represented by Heidegger is of an essentially different kind." [83] But in this hour "when all speech must have a deadly seriousness," Heidegger *takes from us the real encounter of man with God.*

None of these men have fully realized, maintains Buber, that "every religious utterance is a vain attempt to do justice to the meaning which has been attained. All religious expression is only an intimation of its attainment. The reply of the people of Israel on Sinai, 'We will do it, we will hear it,' expresses the decisive with naive and unsurpassable pregnancy. The meaning is found through the engagement of one's own person; it only reveals itself as one takes part in its revelation." [84]

"All religious reality begins with what Biblical religion calls the 'fear of God.' It comes when our existence between birth and death becomes incomprehensible and uncanny, when all security is shattered through the mystery. This is not the relative mystery of that which is inaccessible only to the present state of human knowledge and is hence in principle discoverable. It is the essential mystery, the inscrutableness of which belongs to its very nature; it is the unknowable. Through this dark gate (which is only a gate and not, as some theologians believe, a dwelling) the believing man steps forth into the everyday which is henceforth hallowed as the place in which he has to live with the mystery. He steps forth directed and assigned to the concrete, contextual situations of his existence. That he henceforth accepts the situation as given him by the Giver is what Biblical religion calls the 'fear of God.' " [85]

Symbols of God come into being "when and insofar as Thou becomes He, and that means It." [86] To be sure we need symbols. Without them we cannot speak of God at all. "Symbols supplement one another, they merge, they are set before the community of believers in plastic or theological forms. And God, so we may surmise, does not despise all these similarly and necessarily untrue images, but rather suffers that one look at Him through them. Yet they always quickly desire to be more than they are, more than signs and pointers toward Him. It finally happers ever again that they swell themselves up and obstruct the way to Him, and He removes Himself from them." [87]

III. Modern Thinkers on Buber

We turn now to some of the evaluations of Buber as they are given by various modern thinkers.

Will Herberg

We have already referred to Will Herberg. In his book, *Four Existentialist Theologians*. Herberg puts Buber along side of Jacques Maritain, Nicolas Berdyaev and Paul Tillich. All are called existentialists. Tracing Buber's philosophical ancestry, Herberg says: "He was early influenced by the giants of German idealism and romanticism, and by the German mystics, Meister Eckhart and Jakob Boehme. Hasidism, in both its mystical and existential strains, has permeated his thinking from his youth. But of all nineteenth-century figures, it was Kierkegaard, Dostoevsky, and Nietzsche who, by his own account, meant most to him, and with them, too, his intellectual relations have been complex and many-sided." [88]

In his *Judaism and Modern Man,*[89] "an interpretation of Jewish Religion," Herberg offers Judaism as an answer to modern man's search for the Absolute, and Buber as one of its greatest prophets.

Herberg, as well as Buber, speaks of two mutually exclusive views of religion.[90] There is first the "Hebraic outlook." [91] It believes in "the absolute transcendence of God." [92] There is, second, the Greco-Oriental outlook. According to it "the ultimate reality is some primal impersonal force." [93] One may call it Brahma or, as Spinoza does, "the All-Soul or Nature." With this view we are always on the way to pantheism.[94] There is on the one hand the living God of Hebraism and there is, on the other hand, the God-idea.[95] "God, in Hebraic religion, is an active, living 'decision-making' Being who plunges into history and personally encounters men in their activity." [96] Of course, we must beware of ever simply identifying this God with anything found in this world.[97] God is always sovereign over everything in the world.[98]

The Scriptural account of man "conveys the profound truth of his paradoxical status in the universe. Man is in nature, yet transcends it; he is subject to the rule of natural necessity, yet retains an irreducible freedom of self-determination within the conditioning factors of nature and history." [99] Following this biblical principle Søren Kierkegaard says that Spirit "is self," is personality.[100] Thinking of all this, we see why Buber so often speaks of Spirit as "the word," or rather the capacity of the word, the "capacity to hear and to respond." [101] But this "capacity to hear and to respond" must again not be directly identified with anything found in this world. "The Hebraic view of man is thus irreducibly ambivalent, hinging as it does upon a dramatic tension both in the nature of man and in his relations with God." [102]

Thus the ultimate imperative of Jewish ethics is "the affirmation of the Living God and the repudiation of idolatry." [103] And Buber is, for Herberg, a great defender of the glory of God.[104] Over against the Spinozistic tendency toward Pantheism, Buber defended the true dialogical principle. Over against idealism which knows nothing of the "I-Thou communion of love," Buber defends the true personality of man.[105] Together with such men as Richard Niebuhr and Emil Brunner among Christians, as well as with his fellow-Jew, Franz Rosenweig, Buber has shown "how one may take Scripture with utmost seriousness as the record of revelation while avoiding the pitfalls of fundamentalism." [106] "Revelation is not the communication of infallible information, as the fundamentalists claim, nor is it the outpouring of 'inspired' sages and poets, as the modernists conceive it. *Revelation is the self-disclosure of God in his dealings with the world.*" [107]

According to Herberg, then, we may safely follow Buber as, with existentialism, he leads us back to the true principle of Hebraism and therefore toward to a renewed statement of the dialogical principle. As we do so, we shall also reach out beond the false alternative expressed in the fundamentalist-modernist controversy in religion. Beyond this we shall be ready, when the time comes, for union with those who call themselves Christians, but who, following the lead of Kierkegaard and others are, in reality, committed to a true personalist philosophy which leaves the Christ of Paul out of consideration.

W. Aalders

In 1955 W. Aalders published a little book under the title *Martin Buber*.[108]

Aalders begins by pointing out that Buber, even in his early days, never thought of Athens and Jerusalem as complete contrasts to one another.[109] To be sure, his soul was from his youth steeped in everything Jewish. And he lived in the deep and mystic piety of Hasidism.[110] His early publications deal with this subject.

After the first world war Buber became deeply conscious of his mission. He must interpret the message of Judaism as that in which the true relation of man to man is "rooted in God." [111] The world must see and appreciate the message of the Old Testament.[112] The Jews and the Church need each other.[113] Aalders quotes from Buber on this point from *Zwei Glaubenweisen* (*Two Types of Faith*). Buber tells us of meeting Ragaz who, says Buber, "looked forward to a future understanding between the nuclear community of Israel and a true community of Jesus, an understanding, although as yet inconceivable, which would arise on neither a Jewish nor a Christian basis, but rather on that of the common message of Jesus and the prophets of the turning of man and of the Kingship of God." [114]

It should be noted here that a Christianity which could be visualized as united with a Judaism, in terms of a principle beyond both, is a Christianity from which Paulinism has been excluded. In spite of all the insistence that it is the principle of Judaism that *alone* has the message the world needs today, Buber is willing to go onward to something beyond Judasim.

We have seen that Buber has already *included* the religion of Jesus, as over against that of Paul, into that of Judaism. But even more basic than this is the fact that the principle of Judaism, as Buber describes it, is that of an *open* religion. The only point of view excluded is *fundamentalism,* which is, like Paulinism, insistent on identifying something in this world, namely Christ, as absolute.

Paulinism, Spinozism, and fundamentalism all fail to see that any direct identification of anything in this world with God is idolatry. But all those who postulate God as unknowable by any direct statement about him, and therefore think of all human language, biblical as well as other, as inherently ambiguous, are welcome to join the future communion of Jew and Gentile visualized by Ragaz.

Excommunication. Of particular interest is the question as to whether in such a new communion as is visualized by Ragaz there will be any such thing as excommunication.

The synagogue excommunicated both Spinoza and Sabbatai Svi. That was because they no longer believed the true Jewish principle.

But does not the true Jewish principle teach that in every man there is a "hidden spark of God"? [115] And does not every man have within him the power of conversion toward the truth no matter how far removed from it he may be? Why then should any one be excommunicated from the synagogue?

The answer is that those who were excommunicated violated the basic concept of the Jewish principle in that they found in this world a direct revelation of God.

Such men are "covenant-breakers." Essential to the idea of this breaking of the covenant is the notion that messianic salvation has localized and thus established itself and that faith is to be regarded as a possession of redemptive reality.[116]

In the past Christianity has been insufficiently conscious of its covenant responsibility to be able to take this high view of excommunication. To be sure, the church inherited something of the idea of the covenant.[117] But the church had little resistance against the intrusion of the idea of absolute truth as directly found on earth. Accordingly, the church had little power of inward renewal. It is therefore the glorious task of the Jews to lead the church into the truth of the covenantal relation of God to man.

Basic to the renewal of the church in terms of the true Jewish covenantal idea is therefore a new view of Jesus. "Because the church has proclaimed Jesus to be the divine redeemer, and has worked out this idea into extremes in its Christological and trinitarian teaching, covenant consciousness has been undermined." [118] As the first of many messianic figures within Jewry we may think of him as incomparably the most pure. But we must not make him divine.[119] Excommunication needs to be applied. How else can we keep the communion from being overrun by false Messianism. But excommunication must be applied only to those who break the whole basis of the covenant by their holding to Christ as the Son of God and to the New Testament as his finished revelation.

M. H. Bolkestein

We turn now to the work of M. H. Bolkestein on the *I-Thou Scheme in Recent Philosophy and Theology*.

Bolkestein places Buber, in conjunction with others, as a leader among those who offered in their I-Thou scheme a basic criticism on German idealism.[120] He speaks of F. Ebner, of E. Grisebach, of F. Gogarten, of E. Brunner, of R. Bultmann, together with K. Lowith, of K. Heim, and of K. Barth, as each in his own way seeking, attacking, and rejecting the Ego-concept of Idealism.[121]

The I-Thou scheme intends to bring about a total renewal of thought. It wants to lead into a deeper layer of reality than can be reached by the subject-object scheme.[122] In general, says Bolke-stein, idealism may be said to stand for a process of thinking within the circle of the ego.[123] To begin with Kant, he did not in principle escape the circle of *Icheinsamkeit*.[124] The same holds true for Fichte, *Im Ich Soll Alles Gesetzt Sein*.[125] Hegel's philosophy was mono-logical.[126] It would be of no help to follow Feuerbach in his criticism of idealism. In his case, no less in that of those whose thinking he rejects, man remains by himself.[127] However, with Kierkegaard we have something different. He wants to start from the individual. But his is not an absolute individualism. In his case the "individual is always related to God." [128] Even so, we must go beyond Kierke-gaard. He had no eye as yet for the I-Thou scheme.[129]

In Ebner's *Das Wort und die geistigen Realitäten* (1921), con-tinues Bolkestein, the I-Thou scheme is used. As a Roman Catholic Christian he uses this scheme to his satisfaction.[130] Comes now Martin Buber. His little volume on *Ich und Du* appeared in 1923. "Ebner and Buber have become the 'portal figures' of a new ontology (Cullberg)." [131] For Buber the I must be related to the Thou and the pure Thou is God. God is "das ganz gegenwärtige" (*Ich und Du*, p. 93). Man must not seek to possess God. Nor must he seek to possess himself. God and man exist in mutual interrelation with one another. And this mutual interrelation implies mutual inter-action. Moreover this mutual interaction is of a moment by moment nature. "Revelation is not one content [of thought] next to others." [132]

Bolkestein says that we may call Buber's view "panentheistic" but not pantheistic.[133]

Turning now to Gogarten, we learn that he was the first Protestant theologian to realize the importance of the I-Thou scheme.[134] In his *Glauben und Offerbarung* (1928) he mentions Buber's name with great appreciation.[135] After 1920 Gogarten develops a reformatorial and specifically Lutheran view of faith.[136] Thus he realizes that the reality of man is "die widerspruchsvolle, die gegensätzliche von Du und Ich." [137]

As to Brunner, says Bolkestein, his final approach involves an I-Thou approach.[138] In Brunner's final view, to be man is to be in communion with God.[139] True humanity is attained only in faith.[140] The I-Thou philosophy, therefore, helped Brunner to develop an existentially deepened view of revelation. Revelation for Brunner involves "personal *Korrespondenz*." [141]

As for Bultmann, he too commits himself to the I-Thou scheme.[142] The same holds true for Heim.

Finally Barth must be mentioned. He, more than any of the others, has constructed the I-Thou relation in a strict theological and Christocentric fashion.[143] For him the law springs from the gospel. There is no imperative except on the basis of grace. Only if we regard men in Christ can we address him as *Thou*.[144] "The church is the place of the true I-Thou relation. Under the word of Christ there is true individuality and true communion." [145]

Ludwig Binswanger

In 1953 Ludwig Binswanger published the second edition of his *Grundformen und Erkenntnis Menschlichen Daseins*. In this work Binswanger points out that Buber was a pioneer in the recent movement of thought which realizes that man stands in communion with his fellowman and that it is this communion that makes him man. Ebner and Gogarten are also mentioned in this connection.[146]

Buber, says Binswanger, speaks of "Gegenstande" which lived in the past and of "Wesenheiten" which live in the present.[147] This thought is similar to that of Grisebach who speaks of "zwei sich gegenseitig gegenwartende Personen." [148] For Buber, as for others, it is the love-relation between men that makes them men. Binswanger expresses this idea when he speaks of the "Wir der Liebe" as basic for the understanding of man as man.[149] And this leads to the glorious vision of man's understanding of his task in the spirit of love. Even his task with respect to the world of things is transfigured by the fact that in a common love-relation to one another men work at it together. Buber expressed this idea in *Ich und Du* when he said: "Liebe ist ein welthaftes Wirken. Wer in ihr steht, in ihr schaut, dem lösen sich Menschen aus ihrer Verflochtenheit ins Getriebe; Gute und Böse, Kluge und Törichte, Schöne und Hässliche, einer um den andern wird ihm wirklich und zum Du, das ist losgemacht, herausgetreten, einzig und gegenüber wesend; Ausschliesslichkeit ersteht wunderbar Mal um Mal—und so kann er wirken, helfen, heilen, erziehen, erheben, erlösen." [150]

And though Buber thinks in all this as a theist, and not as a theologian,[151] for him as well as for those who think theologically, this awareness of the We-ness (Wirheit) as a norm gladly accepted for themselves by men, is thought of as a gift.[152]

Maurice S. Friedman

In 1955 Maurice S. Friedman published his comprehensive work, *Martin Buber* with the subtitle *The Life of Dialogue*.[153] We can convey only a very little of the wealth of thought to be found in this book.

Buber sometimes refers to his position as similar to a narrow ridge. By this he wants to make certain that his thought be not considered as a closed system of ideas.[154] Accordingly, faith is not faith in a system of truth to be set over against a system of falsehood.[155] By setting systems of truth as "either-ors" over against one another both truth and life are falsified.[156]

Friedman at once applies the idea of the narrow ridge to the problem of evil. "Buber's system of valuing is so closely connected with the problem of evil that this problem can be used as a unifying centre for his work without doing injustice to the many fields in which he has written." [157]

In our time men reject the "shallow optimism and naive faith in the progress of preceding ages." [158] In contrast with this optimism some men today hold "that evil is absolute and unredeemable." Buber holds to neither extreme. For him evil has reality, but its reality is never permanent nor is it ever completely divorced from the good. Hence it is capable of redemption by the process of the world spirit, the grace of God, or the redemptive activity of man." [159] It is this "middle position between the unreality and the radical reality of evil" that Buber held to at every stage of his development.[160]

In Hasidism, says Friedman, Buber found a congenial atmosphere. For Hasidism evil "is explained as a waste product of creation and an inevitable result of the limitation, or judgment, that must take place if separate things are to exist at all." [161] In Hasidism the origin of evil is explained by the figure of "the breaking of the vessels which contain the divine grace. As a result of the breaking of the vessels, the divine harmony is disrupted, the Shekinah is exiled, and sparks of divinity fall downward into physical creation. In the physical world the sparks are surrounded by hard shells of darkness (*qelipot*), a type of negative evil. This whole process is further confirmed by the fall of man, but it is also within man's power to liberate the divine sparks from their imprisonment in the shells and send them upward again to union with their divine source. Through this liberation the power of darkness is overcome and *tikkum,* the restoration of the original harmony, is effected.

"This restoration in itself causes the redemption of man and the world. Though it cannot be completed by man's action, man can start the movement which God will complete by sending down His grace to the world in the form of the Messiah. For this purpose man must not only observe every injunction of the law but be must practise mystical prayer, and he must bring to his actions and prayers· special types of mystical intention, or *kavanot. Kavanah* represents a deliberate concentration of will, an inner attitude which is far more effective than the particular nature of the action being performed. However, the greatest effectiveness is only secured by the practice of special *kavanot* for each of the different actions. Thus, what was at its best a concern for inward devotion became at its worst an attempt to use magic to bring about the advent of the Messiah.[162]

It can be seen from this statement that Buber's view of evil was, in his earlier days, essentially that of mysticism. "Thus for Buber's early mystical philosophy, evil is equivalent to inner division and separation from the ground of life, and the redemption of evil is the realization of a lived unity which not only removes the dissension in the individual but makes actual the unity and perfection of the world." [163]

But Buber went beyond mysticism. Never a rationalist, he nonetheless sought to combine rational thought and mystical experience. Buber thinks of a society of creative persons who bring about harmony between intellectual thought, mystical experience, and constructive action. Such a society is represented by Judaism.[164] Buber looks toward the future in which men in general will be enthralled with this ideal.[165]

50

In the course of time Buber, therefore, went beyond mysticism to a philosophy of realization. Buber learned from Kant that the realization of man and his ideals cannot be accomplished in terms of the "naive, pre-Kantian 'objective' view of the universe." [166] His teacher, Wilhelm Dilthey, made it perfectly clear to him that such realization must rather be built on the distinction between the spiritual and the natural sciences. Friedrich Nietzsche, too, helped Buber to see the need for "wholeness of being as opposed to detached intellectuality." [167] "Probably the strongest influence on Buber's concept of realization, however, was the existentialist philosophy of Søren Kierkegaard." Buber also owes much to Dostoievsky. [168]

"In addition to Hasidism, Kierkegaard, and Dilthey, the most important influence on the development of Buber's I-Thou philosophy were Ludwig Feuerbach and Georg Simmel. Buber states in 'What Is Man?' that Feuerbach gave him a decisive impetus in his youth. Unlike Kant, writes Buber, Feuerbach postulates the whole man and not cognition as the beginning of philosophizing, and by man he 'does not mean man as an individual, but man with man—the connection of *I* and *Thou*.' " [169]

Having seen that the realization of human personality must take place at the borderline between the realm of science and that of personality, Buber gradually attained to the vision that such realization involves the I-Thou relationship. How do we explain man's "feeling of unity with certain objects of nature"? "In Buber's essay on Jacob Boehme (1900) this feeling of unity is used to illustrate the idea of man as the microcosm, or little world which contains the whole. In 'Ecstasy and Confession' (1909) it is used to illustrate the oneness in ecstasy of the 'I' and the world. In *Daniel* (1913) it is used to illustrate the unity which is created and realized in the world. And in *Ich und Du* (1922) it is used to illustrate the I-Thou relation, an event which takes place between two beings which nonetheless remain separate. Two of the specific experiences which Buber mentions in the essay on Boehme—that of kinship with a tree and that of looking into the eyes of a dumb animal—are later used in *I and Thou* as an example not of unity but of the I-Thou relation. Yet the emotional content of the experiences as described in the two works is almost identical!" [170]

Herewith we have reached Buber's mature philosophy. In his mature view the mystic approach and the idea of realization are not rejected but given a new setting. Buber now realizes that "all real living is meeting." [171] All of human experience is, from the beginning relational. And "pure relation is love *between* the I and the Thou." [172] "Hate sees only a part of being. If a man sees a whole being and still hates, he is no longer in relation but in I-It; for to say Thou to a man means to affirm his being." [173] "To be fully real the I-Thou relation must be mutual." [174]

For many years since his first vision of the I-Thou relation, Buber has applied the principle of dialogue involved in it to many and various aspects of life. Always and everywhere the "narrow ridge" idea has been maintained. Always the question pertains to the "sphere of the between." [175] Those who seek for the true realization of themselves and others may be called "essence-men" (*Wesenmensch*). In contrast with essence-men there are the "image-men" (*Bildmensch*). The essence man is unselfish but the image man "is primarily concerned with what the other thinks of him." [176] Essence-men operate with the principle of love.[177] Of course, love turned upon one's self is evil. It is monological.[178] *True love is dialogical.*

IV. The Nature of Evil

Herewith we return to the question of evil and how it may be removed from the heart of man and from society.

"It is entering into relation that makes man really man . . . ." And it is failure to enter into relation that in the last analysis constitutes evil. . . ." [179]

In his *Images of Good and Evil,* Buber has come to full maturity with respect to the question of evil.[180] The first stage of evil is decisionlessness. "When Adam and Eve take the fruit, they do not make a decision between good and evil but rather imagine possibilities of action and then act almost without knowing it, sunk in a 'strange and dreamlike kind of contemplation.' " [181] "Man grasps at every possibility 'in order to overcome the tension of omnipossibility' and thus makes incarnate a reality which is 'no longer divine but his, his capriciously constructed, indestinate reality.' It is this, in the story of the Flood, which causes God to repent of having made man. The wickedness of man's actions does not derive from a corruption of the soul but from the intervention of the evil 'imagery.' " [182]

52

As to the question of inherited sin Buber holds that "the 'evil-urge' is especially close to the 'imagery of man's heart' which the Bible speaks of as 'evil from his youth,' for it is identical with 'passion, that is, the power peculiar to man, without which he can neither beget nor bring forth, but which, left to itself, remains without direction and leads astray.' " [183]

The second stage of evil, "the actual decision to evil," may be interpreted with the help of Zoroastrian myths. "The primal spirits stand between God and man and like them choose between good and evil. But in the case of Ahriman, the evil spirit, this choice takes place in pure paradox since in choosing he acknowledges himself precisely as the evil." [184]

The Eclipse of God

"The absolute affirmation of the self in the second stage of evil is an extreme form of man's hiding from the 'signs' which address him.[185] But "a more common form of cutting oneself off from dialogue" is to develop a system of doctrines with respect to God and his relation to man.[186] "The 'once for all' of dogma resists the unforeseeable moment and thereby becomes 'the most exalted form of invulnerability against revelation.' " [187] "It is only one step from dogma to 'magic' for a God that can be fixed in dogma can also be possessed and used." [188]

From such great sin man can always turn back to God. "Man's turning from evil and taking the direction toward God is the beginning of his own redemption and that of the world." [189] "The *teshuvah,* or turning to God, is born in the depths of the soul out of 'the despair which shatters the prison of our latent energies' and out of the suffering which purifies the soul." [190] Of course, "the belief in the redemption of evil does not mean any security of salvation." [191] There is always "the cruel opposition of existence itself." [192]

We end this section of Friedman's analysis by observing his understanding of Buber's theory of knowledge.

"Human truth is participation in Being, not conformity between a proposition and that to which the proposition refers. It cannot claim universal validity yet it can be exemplified and symbolized in actual life."

V. Evaluation

We look first at the evaluations of Buber's thought as given by Herberg, Aalders, Bolkestein, Binswanger, and Friedman. After that we conclude with some remarks about Buber's thought and its relation to Christianity.

Will Herberg. The position of Herberg is obviously similar to that of Buber and largely dependent upon it. As such, his position needs no further analysis. Herberg has helped us by placing Buber in a class with Maritain, Berdyaev, and Tillich, as one of the representatives of modern existentialism.

W. Aalders. From Aalders we learn especially the importance of Buber's thought for the new ecumenical community. Every modern Protestant as well as Roman Catholic is welcomed into it by Buber; only the believer in the direct revelation of God in Christ is excluded. It is this new community centered about the idea of loyalty by good men to God as the ideal limit of love that will accomplish the redemption of the world.

M. H. Bolkestein. Bolkestein shows that in his I-Thou scheme Buber is trying to escape the internal circularity of idealist thinking. Bolkestein shows that the I-Thou scheme is so flexible as to be able to serve as a foundation either for a Christ-centered position like that of Barth or as the foundation for Jewish Messianism. This is due to its basically *ethical* thrust.

Ludwig Binswanger. Binswanger stresses the idea that Buber, together with many other modern thinkers, holds to the principle of love as that which enables men to approach one another as truly personal. Man is essentially the being who loves God and who is loved by God.

Maurice S. Friedman. Friedman ties together the various stages of Buber's thought and enables us to see that they reach their climax in the idea of the true man (*Wesensmensch*) as over against the image-man (*Bildmensch*) as redeeming himself by his conversion to God from all that which lacks direction within him.

These five men have helped us to understand Buber. They have all placed his philosophical thinking as representative of a high or spiritual type of existentialism. Buber's is a form of existentialism that opposes other forms of existentialism, such as that of Sartre.

These men have all seen the significance of Buber's philosophy, together with that of the modern Protestant followers of Kant and Kierkegaard, as a proper foundation for the church of the future. The Jewish principle is consonant with modern philosophy and theology so far as these are based on the primacy of the *practical* reason.

It is, however, almost exclusively by indirection that any of these men give any indication of the basic relation of Buber's thinking to Christianity. The *basic* relation, as earlier indicated, is that of complete rejection. Buber speaks, of course, of Jesus as his brother. He even speaks of him as one of, or, beyond that, the *most important* of a series of Messiahs. But this only indicates that for Buber, Jesus is not his Lord. For Buber, Jesus is not the Son of God. When Jesus said that he and the Father were one, this is, for Buber, no less than for the Pharisess, nothing less than blasphemy.

But through his mysticism, through his idea of self-realization and through his I-Thou philisophy, Buber has made common cause with Neo-Protestantism and, to an extent, with modern Roman Catholicism. Together they stand for a theology that is consonant with Kant's idea of the primacy of the practical reason. Together they believe that human knowledge of the field of science is of an impersonal sort. What they speak of as the I-It dimension is roughly equivalent to what Kant spoke of as the phenomenal world, the world of causal relations.

For Buber, as for Kant before him, the human self, as free, stands above this I-It dimension. This other dimension is that of free or autonomous personality. It is in this realm of autonomous personality that man meets his fellow-man. It is here, too, that he meets his God. Man knows nothing of his God in any conceptual way. The God of the existentialists and the God of the I-Thou philosophers, including Buber, hold to the idea of the unknown and unknowable God. If anything is clear it is that according to Kant man can say *nothing* intellectually about God. It is only on the basis of his moral sense that man, knowing nothing of God, must nonetheless postulate not only his existence, but also his governance over the I-It dimension.

Buber seeks to relate, if not, identify, this modern ethical dualism turned ethical monism with the concept of the covenantal relation between God and man that is found in the Old Testament.

In order to effect this combination or virtual identification of modern existentialism with the Old Testament idea of the covenant Buber does, in effect, what Philo did in his day, namely, allegorize the history of redemption as the Old Testament teaches it. The relation of God to man and the world, the relation of man to God and the world is reduced to a correlativity between a rationalist principle of continuity which combines by identification and an irrationalist principle which separates by complete disconnection. If God were to be known at all he would have to be exhaustively known and since he is not exhaustively known he is not known at all. Yet, though he is not known at all, he is still exhaustively known. God is always at the same time both wholly known and wholly unknown.

We cannot think that with such a philosophy Buber, any more than other I-Thou philosophers or any more than other existentialists, has espaced the *Icheinsamkeit* that they rightly found in Idealism.

The final reference point in Buber's thought is the "free"man. Buber can find no adequate words of scorn to describe the idea of Paul that God in Christ sovereignly creates and redeems men. The Old Testament Genesis account of the origin of man and of the first sin of man is simply rejected as being out of accord with the idea of human freedom and of human goodness. For Buber it is not the plan of God but abstract possibility that constitutes man's original environment. For Buber it is not God who speaks through Moses giving his covenant people the law. For Buber physical law is the idea of regularity imposed upon chance-existence by the mind of man for his practical purposes. For Buber moral law is that which the free and good man sets forth before himself as ideals according to which he would regulate human society.

All in all, we have in the thinking of Buber a covenant philosophy and theology which is built on man instead of on God as its source. This apostate covenant theology would envelop and thereby destroy the covenant theology of the Old Testament of which Christ is the center. So far as the ecumenical Christian church accepts the leadership of Buber in its view of *love* as *the* relation between men which really makes them men, the love of God for sinners has disappeared. So far as theology follows Buber in thinking of the universe as sacramental it has, in effect, denied the efficacy of the sacrament of the Lord's supper as the ordinance of Christ that binds the redeemed both body and soul to their Redeemer.

56

NOTES

1. Martin Buber, *Two Types of Faith* (tr. Norman P. Goldhawk; New York: Harper & Brothers, 1961), p. 12.
2. *Ibid.*, pp. 12-13.
3. *Ibid.*, p. 12.
4. *Ibid.*, p. 11.
5. *Ibid.*, p. 7.
6. *Ibid.*
7. *Ibid.*, p. 12.
8. *Ibid.*, p. 32.
9. *Ibid.*, p. 37.
10. *Ibid.*, p. 38.
11. *Ibid.*, p. 39.
12. *Ibid.*, p. 44.
13. *Ibid.*
14. *Ibid.*
15. *Ibid.*, p. 46.
16. *Ibid.*
17. *Ibid.*
18. *Ibid.*, p. 47.
19. *Ibid.*
20. *Ibid.*
21. *Ibid.*, p. 49.
22. *Ibid.*, p. 50.
23. *Ibid.*, p. 51.
24. *Ibid.*
25. *Ibid.*
26. *Ibid.*, p. 52.
27. *Ibid.*, p. 55.
28. *Ibid.*, p. 64.
29. *Ibid.*, p. 57.
30. *Ibid.*
31. *Ibid.*, p. 58.
32. *Ibid.*, p. 61.
33. *Ibid.*, pp. 63-64.
34. *Ibid.*, p. 79.
35. *Ibid.*, p. 80.
36. *Ibid.*
37. *Ibid.*, p. 81.
38. *Ibid.*, p. 47.
39. *Ibid.*, p. 81.
40. *Ibid.*, p. 84.
41. *Ibid.*, p. 86.

42. *Ibid.*, p. 89.

43. *Ibid.*

44. *Ibid.*

45. *Ibid.*, pp., 89-90.

46. *Ibid.*, p. 90.

47. *Ibid.*, p. 128.

48. *Ibid.*

49. *Ibid.*, p. 130.

50. Martin Buber, *Between Man and Man* (tr. Ronald Gregor Smith; New York: The Macmillan Co., 1948), p. vii.

51. *Ibid.*, p. 5.

52. *Ibid.*, p. 6.

53. *Ibid.*

54. Will Herberg, *Four Existentialist Theologians* (Garden City: Doubleday & Company, Inc. 1957), p. 9.

55. *Ibid.*, p. 10.

56. *Ibid.*, p. 56.

57. Martin Buber, *The Origin and Meaning of Hasidism* (ed. and tr. Maurice Friedman; New York: Horizon Press, 1960), p. 90.

58. *Ibid.*

59. *Ibid.*, p. 91.

60. *Ibid.*, p. 92.

61. *Ibid.*

62. *Ibid.*

63. *Ibid.*, p. 93.

64. *Ibid.*

65. *Ibid.*, p. 99.

66. *Ibid.*, p. 100.

67. *Ibid.*, p. 101.

68. *Ibid.*, p. 102.

69. *Ibid.*, p. 104.

70. *Ibid.*, p. 105.

71. *Ibid.*, p. 107.

72. *Ibid.*, pp. 109-110.

73. *Ibid.*, pp. 111-112.

74. Martin Buber, *Eclipse of God* (New York: Harper & Brothers, 1952).

75. *Ibid.*, p. 15.

76. *Ibid.*, p. 18.

77. *Ibid.*

78. *Ibid.*, p. 19.

79. *Ibid.*

80. *Ibid.*, p. 20.

81. *Ibid.*

82. Ibid., p. 21.

83. *Ibid.*

84. *Ibid.*, p. 36a.

85. *Ibid.*, p. 36b.
86. *Ibid.*, p. 45.
87. *Ibid.*, pp. 45-46.
88. Herberg, *op. cit.*, p. 174.
89. Will Herberg, *Judaism and Modern Man* (New York: Meridian Books, Inc., 1959).
90. *Ibid.*, p. 55.
91. *Ibid.*, p. 49.
92. *Ibid.*, p. 48.
93. *Ibid.*
94. *Ibid.*
95. *Ibid.*, p. 58.
96. *Ibid.*, p. 62.
97. *Ibid.*
98. *Ibid.*, p. 64.
99. *Ibid.*, p. 69.
100. *Ibid.*, p. 71.
101. *Ibid...*
102. *Ibid.*, p. 75.
103. *Ibid.*, p. 96.
104. *Ibid.*, p. 139.
105. *Ibid.*, p. 205.
106. *Ibid.*, p. 246.
107. *Ibid.*
108. W. Aalders, *Martin Buber* (Utrecht).
109. *Ibid.*, p. 7.
110. *Ibid.*, p. 8.
111. *Ibid.*, p. 9.
112. *Ibid.*, p. 10.
113. *Ibid.*
114. Buber, *Two Types of Faith, op. cit.*, p. 15.
115. Aalders, *op. cit.*, p. 23.
116. *Ibid.*, p. 35.
117. *Ibid.*, p. 37.
118. *Ibid.*, p. 38.
119. *Ibid.*
120. M. H. Bolkestein, *Het Ik-Gij Schema in de Nieuwere Philosophie en Theologie* (Wageningen: H. Veenman & Zonen, 1941), p. 3.
121. *Ibid.*, p. 3.
122. *Ibid.*
123. *Ibid.*, p. 5.
124. *Ibid.*, p. 7.
125. *Ibid.*, p. 8.
126. *Ibid.*, p. 11.
127. *Ibid.*, p. 15.
128. *Ibid.*, p. 17.

129. *Ibid.*
130. *Ibid.*, p. 24.
131. *Ibid.*, p. 30.
132. *Ibid.*, p. 39.
133. *Ibid.*
134. *Ibid.*, p. 59.
135. *Ibid.*
136. *Ibid.*, p. 61.
137. *Ibid.*, p. 65.
138. *Ibid.*, p. 103.
139. *Ibid.*, p. 104.
140. *Ibid.*, p. 111.
141. *Ibid.*, p. 117.
142. *Ibid.*, p. 121.
143. *Ibid.*, p. 164.
144. *Ibid.*
145. *Ibid.*, p. 165.
146. Ludwig Binswanger, *Grundformen und Erkenntnis Menschlichen Daseins* (Zurich, 1953), p. 16. Cf. p. 122 for reference to Ebner.
147. *Ibid.*, p. 47.
148. *Ibid.*
149. *Ibid.*, p. 90.
150. *Ibid.*, p. 99.
151. *Ibid.*, p. 122.
152. *Ibid.*, p. 137.
153. Maurice S. Friedman, *Martin Buber, Life of Dialogue* (Chicago: University of Chicago Press, 1956).
154. *Ibid.*, p. 3.
155. *Ibid.*, p. 5.
156. *Ibid.*, p. 4.
157. *Ibid.*, p. 12.
158. *Ibid.*, p. 13.
159. *Ibid.*, p. 14.
160. *Ibid.*
161. *Ibid.*, p. 18.
162. *Ibid.*
163. *Ibid.*, p. 30.
164. *Ibid.*, p. 31.
165. *Ibid.*, p. 32.
166. *Ibid.*, p. 34.
167. *Ibid.*, p. 35.
168. *Ibid.*
169. *Ibid.*, p. 48.
170. *Ibid.*, p. 49.
171. *Ibid.*, p. 57.

172. *Ibid.*, p. 59.
173. *Ibid.*
174. *Ibid.*, p. 61.
175. *Ibid.*, p. 85.
176. *Ibid.*, pp. 85-86.
177. *Ibid.*, p. 88.
178. *Ibid.*, p. 89.
179. *Ibid.*, p. 101.
180. *Ibid.*
181. *Ibid.*, p. 105.
182. *Ibid.*
183. *Ibid.*, pp. 105-106.
184. *Ibid.*, p. 107.
185. *Ibid.*, p. 113.
186. *Ibid.*
187. *Ibid.*
188. *Ibid.*
189. *Ibid.*, p. 133.
190. *Ibid.*, p. 134.
191. *Ibid.*, p. 135.
192. *Ibid.*, p. 150.

CHAPTER III

THE TORAH

In the previous chapter we dealt chiefly with Martin Buber and his I-thou philosophy. Buber thinks that by means of his I-thou philosophy he has given the "Jewish principle" a modern expression. But is this really the case? Is not the Jewish principle to be understood basically by studying *The Torah*? Could it be that Buber has made his ready alliance with modern post-Kantian philosophy just because he did not built his thought exclusively on the concept of the Torah? Then is it not historically better to begin a discussion of Jewish apologetics with the place of the Torah? Are not the Jews as the chosen people of God the defenders of his special revelation to mankind? Is it not this that, more than anything else, distinguishes them from all other men?

If the Jews are the true monotheists in the world, surely they are such, not because of a special wisdom that is in them in distinction from other men, but because the true God spoke to them by Moses his prophet! Only those who are true in life and teaching to this revelation really represent the Jewish principle! Why then begin with a modern Jew like Buber?

Our answer to this question will become clear as we take up the traditional Jewish concept of the Torah. In doing so we shall see a basic continuity between traditional Judaism and Martin Buber.

To get under way we follow the work of R. Travers Herford on *Talmud and Apocrypha*.[1] Herford is concerned to show that between the time of Ezra and Jesus there were two movements of thought within Judaism. There was first the movement of thought represented by the apochryphal and pseudepigraphal writings. In these writings there is great stress on apocalyptic matter.

63

There was second the movement of Rabbinical teaching, at first oral and afterwards collected and written down in the Talmud and the Midrash. In this Rabbinical teaching the great stress is on ethics rather than on apocalypti.

"Here then are two great bodies of teachings, the Apocryphal (and Apocalyptic) and the Rabbinical, sharply contrasted while yet both had their ultimate source in the Old Testament, and both were developed side by side with apparently little, if any, contact of one with the other." [2]

New Christian scholars have, says Herford, "extolled the Apocryphal writings as being representative of the ancient free prophetic spirit." R. H. Charles speaks of these writings as the "true child of prophecy."[3] These same Christian scholars tend to think of the Rabbinical literature as "hard and narrow." Herford is out to show that while both lines of teaching spring from a common stock, namely the Old Testament, it is the Rabbinical view that represents the Judaistic view, and especially its high ethical spirit at its best.

I. The Torah and the Old Testament

The name Torah first referred to the Pentateuch and, though the meaning of the word was later greatly extended, "it did not lose and has never lost its primary connexion with the Pentateuch, even down to the present day." [4]

Central to the Torah are the Ten Commandments. And along with them "must be mentioned the great declaration (Deuteronomy 6:4-7), 'Hear, O Israel, the Lord our God, the Lord is one; and thou shalt love the Lord thy God with all thy heart and with all thy soul and with all thy might,' etc. That passage, known from its first word as the Shema, sounds the keynote of all Judaism, and has been its watchword through all the centuries of its existence. It is contained in Deuteronomy, and that book in its ethical teaching may be said to amplify the central thought of the Shema." [5] Words similar to the Shema are found in Leviticus 19:2, "Ye shall be holy, for I the Lord your God am holy."

We are therefore concerned with the Torah and in what it says of God and his ethical requirements for man.

64

II. The Advancing Ethical Consciousness

The Torah is, of course, "invested with divine authority." But, obviously, "some of its contents were ethically higher than others." In this fact of inequality the "advancing ethical consciousness" had its task mapped out for itself.[6]

"The Torah, as the primary source of ethical teaching, offered all that it contained to all who studied it, and they naturally drew from it that to which their own ethical consciousness responded." [7]

In addition to the Torah the Jews of the latest of pre-Christian centuries also recognized the Prophets "as a body of Holy Scripture; but it does not follow, and it was not to be expected that this second collection was placed on an equal level with the Torah. That was never done in Jewish tradition. When once the Torah had been made the supreme authority, there obviously could not be a second supreme authority beside it." [8]

Finally, there were the Hagiographa (*Kethubim*), which were made the third division of the canon and thus a source of later teaching.

When we look at some of the books included in this third division of the canon we are surprised that they were taken into the canon at all. For instance, "it would be hard to find a writer who touched a lower level, in respect of the nobler qualities of the Jewish mind, than the author of Ecclesiastes." [9]

As for Daniel it is "the only avowedly Apocalyptic book in the Canon." [10] It is therefore the ethical rather than the apocalyptic teaching of the Old Testament that supplies the main source of teaching for Judaism. We turn now to this ethical teaching.

The Development Along the Rabbinical Line

To trace the development of the Rabbinical line of teaching and its high ethical attainment means to start with Ezra.

For centuries Israel had lived as though the Torah had never been given them. "The Torah was forgotten in Israel." The exile was God's punishment upon his people for this forgetting of his way. Ezra saw that "the people must obey the teaching already divinely given, and obey it with a deliberate intention which they had never shown before." [11] In the "great assembly," of which

Nehemiah speaks, was signed a covenant promising to obey the Torah anew. Practice did not readily follow theory. Ezra wanted a voluntary acceptance of the Torah. Even so, with the signing of the covenant Judaism was born.

The Sopherim

After Ezra came a group of men who carried on the intent of his work. These followers of Ezra taught and interpreted the Torah in order to make its authority effective, and thus to carry out the intention of Ezra.[12] To call these men jurists or doctors of the law would be misleading "if only because the Torah is not Law." [13] They were simply teachers of the Torah.

Tradition speaks of the Great Synagogue as existing at a time soon after Ezra. The purpose of this body was to carry on the work of Ezra, and the tradition.[14] We may then think of the Sopherim and the men of the great synagogue as referring to the same entity.

The Torah had been given "for the guidance and instruction of Israel." [15] But not all the people could interpret the Torah for themselves. It had to be done for them. And this work of interpreting the Torah was the task of the Sopherim.[16]

"The form in which that teaching was given was a sort of running commentary on the text, in which the particular lesson or precept which the teacher desired to give was connected with a particular passage of Scripture, and the two always taught together. This is what is meant by Midrash—or, rather, this form of exposition is called the Midrash form in which the precept was given without reference to any passage of Scripture. The Mishnah form was not used by the Sopherim; they used only the Midrash form, which, however, was never abandoned even when the Mishnah form came into use." [17]

The Torah had a non-preceptive as well as a preceptive side. "The distinction between the preceptive and the non-preceptive portions of the Torah is fundamental in that type of Judaism which is represented by the Sopherim, their later successors the Tannaim, and the Talmud and Midrashim generally. Interpretation of the Torah had for its purpose the elucidation of its meaning on both of these sides; and the two forms of interpretation, and more par-

66

ticularly the results obtained by interpretation along both those lines, were indicated by special names—on the preceptive side by Halachah, on the non-preceptive side by Haggadah." [18]

It was "almost a matter of course that the interpretation of the Torah should lay the chief stress upon the halachah, because to *do* the will of God was essential and was within the competence of everyone. But it was no less a matter of course that the haggadah, the interpretation of the non-preceptive side, should be developed side by side with the halachah, because the non-preceptive portions of the Torah were just as truly divine teaching as the preceptive, and it was just as much a duty to learn what was so taught. But there was this difference between them, that the haggadah was not defined in precise terms as the halachah was, it was given not as a rule but as a suggestion, an illustration, and explanation; it was directed not to the will but to the understanding and the imagination. And this explains why the ethical teaching of the Rabbis, following the Sopherim, was given mainly in the form of haggadah." [19]

This distinction between the halachah and haggadah shows at once why "there never has been in Judaism any declaration of belief holding the same position as the Creed holds in the Christian religion." [20] "There were indeed certain limits beyond which a Jew could not go and still remain a Jew." [21] One of these was the Unity of God. But within these limits "belief was free."

We turn now to a consideration of the ethical principles thus evolved. The Sopherim gave little more than a simple exposition of Scripture.[22] They instructed the people orally.[23] In all likelihood they did this regularly.[24]

III. The Unwritten Torah

Herewith we come to the question of the Unwritten Torah. This point is of basic importance. "The period of the Sopherim, or the Great Synagogue, came to an end with the death of Simeon the Just, 270 B.C. But their work, as teachers of the Torah, did not pass away, and the principles which they laid down, as above described, were carried further by a later succession of teachers who eventually became the Rabbis, and whose monument is the Talmud. The duty of teaching the people to know the Torah and to live in accordance with it, continued to be in their hands, as it had been in those of the Sopherim; and the difference between the Sopherim and their later successors was one of method, not of principle. To interpret the Torah was, and always remained, the object in view; but the later teachers developed method of interpretation unknown to the Sopherim, and probably did so from a deeper understanding of the real significance of their work than the Sopherim had ever possessed. It will therefore be necessary to study these further developments along what for brevity I have called the Rabbinical line, so that we may understand the forms in which the teachers of that line gave their instruction, and may be able to form some estimate of the contents of that teaching, especially on the ethical side." [25]

We now see a tradition of Rabbinical teaching established and taught. "There is this difference between the teaching given on the Rabbinical line and that which is contained in the books of the Apocrypha and Pseudepigrapha, that the Rabbinical teaching was given in the form of halachah and haggadah, in accordance with a definite purpose of interpreting the Torah, and based upon a definite conception of what the Torah was and for what end it had been given. The instruction on these lines was the result of the labours of many generations of teachers, all directed to a common end. The teaching of the Apocryphal and Pseudepigraphic books, on the contrary, was the teaching of the individual writers of these books, allowing for the fact that in the case of some of the books, e.g., Enoch, several writers of different dates have been at work." [26]

Let us now trace briefly the "course of development of the oral teaching after the period of the Sopherim, so as to link it on to the Rabbis of the Talmud." [27]

The period of the Sopherim came to an end with the death of Simeon the Just, 270 B.C. Their work was later carried forth by a succession of teachers "who eventually became the Rabbis." [28] In 196 B.C. the Sanhedrin was established "to be the great Council of the Jewish people." [29] Now a "teaching body of some kind began to function in the early years of the Sanhedrin, and developed into the Rabbincal schools of a later age without a break. The names of successive teachers, in pairs (zugoth), are mentioned in the Mishnah (Aboth i. 3-12; Peah ii. 6); and the first pair, Jose b. Joezer of Zeredah and Jose b. Johanan of Jerusalem, were certainly living in the early years of the Sanhedrin. Probably they were members of it, though not the president and vice-president as the Mishnah represents them. They would presumably be the leaders, in the Sanhedrin, of those who were concerned to defend the Torah against the influence of Hellenism, and to maintain its authority amongst the people." [30]

In carrying on the work of the Sopherim these Rabbinisal teachers introduced "an innovation which became of vast importance for the later Judaism. In appearance it was hardly more than a technicality of discussion; in reality it involved a new conception of what the Torah essentially was, and it made possible the continual advance and development through the centuries of the religion which was founded on the Torah. It affected the quality (and incidentially the quantity) of all the teaching which was given in the form of interpretation of Torah, especially on the side of halachah, but also on that of haggadah." [31]

The innovation Herford here discusses has to do with the introduction of the idea of the *Unwritten* Torah. It will be remembered that the Mishna form "states the halachah without any Scripture text to serve as its basis; it merely declares that the halachah is so and so, and the importance of its adoption, along with the Midrash-form which was never abandoned, lies in the fact that it made possible the release of the halachah from the letter of Scripture, sometimes even cutting the connexion altogether." [32]

The principle of the Unwritten Torah enabled the Rabbis to assert divine sanction "for the new customs and practices that had established themselves in the community, at all events such as involved religious acts, which would have been the subject of a halachah in the more orderly time of the Sopherim, and which ought to be the subject of a halachah now, if only some means could be found of ascertaining it." [33] "Or, to put it less technically, some new practice of a religious nature was deemed worthy of approval in itself, was such as to make it highly desirable to recognise it as proper practice for Jews; but the authority of the Torah was the only authority admitted in Jewish religious life since the time of Ezra, and unless the new usage could be brought under the sanction of the Torah, it could make no claim to be accepted, still less declared to be binding. How then could that sanction be given to it so that it might become the subject of a valid halachah? The answer which was found to that question was virtually this:

That the practice in question (whatever it may have been) was evidently a right and good one for Jews to follow; and the fact that they had followed it for an unknown length of time, so that it was now established, might be taken to indicate that there really was a tradition enjoining that practice although there was not a word about it in the written text of the Torah. If this was so, then this tradition must have a certain authority of its own; and, since there could not be two supreme authorities, it followed that the Torah contained more than was set forth in the written text. In other words there must be, and must always have been, an Unwritten Torah alongside of the written one, not as its rival nor even its commentary, but so that the two together, written and unwritten, constituted *the* Torah as it essentially was. To the Sopherim, as to Ezra himself, the Torah had been the written text of the Pentateuch, and the interpretation of it had taken the course of simple explanation in Midrash-form as shown above." [34]

The reader may here stop to catch his breath. What has become of the Torah as a once for all, finished revelation of God to man? In practice it has been reduced to a form. If Protestants are on good ground when they complain of the subjectivism introduced into the church when Roman Catholicism established the idea of tradition as a second source of revelation next to the Scripture, then they are certainly on good ground when they complain of Judaism on the same point. The far-reaching significance of this point will appear again and again. For the moment it must suffice to suggest that the Jews and Jesus clashed precisely on this point. For the Jews the Old Testament and its ordinances had become a form that would contain any content that respectable men might care to put into it. For Jesus the Old Testament continued to be the direct concrete revelation of God to his people centering in its promise with respect to himself.

For the moment, however, we must understand, as Herford informs us, that the Rabbis see the Torah as a pure form with the content that the progressive ethical consciousness of enlightened Jews put into it.

Herford justifies the concept of the Unwritten Torah without hesitation. The idea of the Unwritten Torah, he says, has its weaknesses. Those who advocated it "knew that it cut the connexion between halachah and the written Torah, and they knew that in appearance, at all events, it gave the teachers free scope to teach what they thought fit. Lauterbach has pointed out (*op. cit.,* p. 88) that the Rabbis were rather shy of discussing the basis of their theory, because it would give an opening to their opponents. And, in fact, it was precisely on this question that the Sadducees and the Pharisees were fundamentally divided. The Pharisees maintained the authority of the Unwritten Torah and the Sadducees denied it. (See the present writer's *Pharisees,* p. 64f. and *passim.*)" [35]

"But in spite of its weakness," Herford continues, "or rather its liability to be misrepresented, those who advocated the theory of the Unwritten Torah clung firmly to it, and were fully justified by the results which followed its adoption. The difference which it made was this: That it transformed the Torah from being only a written document already ancient and in danger of becoming obsolete into a continuous revelation keeping pace with the ages, and it threw upon the teachers the responsibility of giving, as Torah, that which in their own mind and conscience was the highest, truest, and best. Of the written Torah the *litera scripta manet*; but as time went on it become more and more difficult to fulfil its precepts to the letter, and the text was overloaded with interpretations (midrash), and supplemented more and more frequently by ordinances (gezeroth) of the priests, directions given for this or that occasion and for which it was never claimed that they were Torah. It was mainly in the Temple and by the priests that the written Torah could still be literally obeyed and its precepts fulfilled. The religious life of the people tended to become more and more dissociated from the written Torah; and if the process had gone on, Judaism as the religion of the Torah would actually have become what it never did become, but what many people imagine that it did, a purely priestly religion, a mere affair of ritual and sacrifices. From such a fate Judaism was saved by the magnificent conception of the Unwritten Torah, and by the faithful devotion of those who worked out that conception, and who steadfastly adhered to the higher and avoided the lower interpretation of which it was capable. They recaptured the idea of religion as the service of the living God, present now as he always had been present to his people, revealing himself now as he had revealed himself to the prophets, and speaking not alone in the words of an ancient text, but in words which came from the

71

heart and conscience of men who felt his hand laid upon them to 'guide them into all truth.' " [36]

The reader may again stop for breath. He can see at a glance that the concept of "continuous revelation" such as the Unwritten Torah advocates is essentially identical with the view of revelation entertained by modern Protestantism. Judaism, Roman Catholicism and modern Protestantism are seen to stand together on the question of the nature of revelation. Martin Buber did nothing more than adopt the language of those who live in terms of the freedom-nature scheme of Kant in order in it to express the rabbinic notion of unwritten law. Moreover, when modern Protestantism begins its journey from Kant to the hermeneutics of recent existentialism it is seen to have its prefiguration in the story of the development of rabbinical theory in ethics. Ethics is what the ethical consciousness of man resolves the good to be regardless of the revelation of the God who speaks by his Son through Moses and the prophets.

The issue between Jesus and the Pharisees is therefore not that between outwardness and inwardness. It is rather between two kinds of inwardness. In the last analysis Jesus asked men to turn away from themselves to God the Father through him. True unity of personality comes only to him who has true unity of purpose in serving God through Christ. Over against this God-centered inwardness to which Jesus came to save men, the Pharisees advocated the man-centered inwardness that is natural to man since his fall in Adam.

All these matters will come up for fuller discussion. We mention them at this juncture so that the real tendency of Jewish thought at this formative period may appear.

IV. Adjustments of the Torah

It is well now to go on with a brief statement of Herford's argument. To us this argument establishes the point just made, namely, that those who refuse to come to God through Christ, in effect, set God as well as Christ aside.

Those who follow the Unwritten Torah do, says Herford, essentially the same thing that the prophets did when "they declared as true and right what their reason and conscience compelled them to own as the highest. That they gave their teaching forth in the form of halachah and haggadah, and not in the form of prophetic oracles, is a difference of method, not of essence." [37]

72

The followers of the Unwritten Torah were engaged in "translating prophecy into the terms of Torah." [38] What then remains of the Torah, we ask. Nothing but a form. The ethical consciousness decides what is right and wrong. This ethical consciousness thinks of itself as being prophetic in exactly the same way that the Old Testament prophets were prophetic. There was nothing left for the Torah to say. There was nothing left that the Torah could have said.

There is, says Herford, "a curious saying in the Talmud (b. B. Bath. 12a), 'Prophecy was taken from the Prophets and was given to the Wise,' to which is added the remark: 'and it had not been taken from these.' That saying was the utterance of a Rabbi of the third century A.D., long after the period with which we are concerned; but it was assumed as an axiom in a discussion which certain still later Rabbis held concerning it." [39]

"The difference between a prophet and a wise man was that the former gave no reason for what he said, while the latter gave a reason, his understanding being enlightened, so as to comprehend what he uttered. The prophet was like a blind man. The relevance of this passage to the subject at present under discussion is that the Rabbis felt that they had, no less but even more than the prophets, divine authority for what they taught, and that this was given to them after the time when the prophets had ceased to function. It was a way of expressing the belief that the revelation did not cease with the extinction of prophecy." [40]

That the idea of an Unwritten Torah is central to Rabbinical Judaism is now established. When the wise men were said to walk in the light of God's countenance they were, if fact, walking in the light of their own enlightened consciousness.

When the Psalmist said, "Open thou mine eyes, that I may behold wondrous things out of thy Torah" he meant that the enlightened ethical consciousness must seek beyond the letter to the meaning of the law. Thus "the conception of the Unwritten Torah is the key to all the subsequent development of Judaism along the Rabbinical line; indeed, without it there could hardly have been any development. What it did was to make possible an ethical advance in the teaching given, not merely by putting a higher construction on older teaching of less ethical worth, but by actually annulling an express command in the written Torah and replacing it by a halachah in

73

accordance with a higher moral standard. This was done in regard
to the famous law 'An eye for an eye', etc. (Exod. 21: 24-5),
which was commuted to a money fine (M. B. Kamma viii. 1).
So in many other instances. The whole tendency was to re-shape
the halachah in accordance with the higher moral standard of those
who from age to age were entrusted with the responsibility of fixing
and declaring it." [41]

V. The Revolt Against Hellenism

There is no need of illustrating the consequences that followed
from the adoption of the Unwritten Torah any further into details.
It is of greater import to see what Herford says about the revolt
against Hellenism that was made in the name of Torah.

One wonders that there was any revolt at all. The ethical consciousness of Rabbinical Judaism had by the time of the Maccabean
revolt already lost every reason for resisting Hellenism. The ethical
consciousness of the Greeks had reached a large measure of inwardness in the person of Socrates. How could Moses challenge Socrates?
Certainly not if he had to speak through the mouth of rabbinical
Judaism. The men of the Unwritten Torah had silenced the voice
of Moses by "internalizing" him. If Moses was to speak to Socrates
through the mouth of the Judaistic prophets he could only urge him
to go forward in his already undertaken path of internalizing the
goal, the standard, and the motivation of ethics. Why should not
Socrates challenge Moses? Who should speak first? Whichever one
was further along on the way to Kant!

It is no surprise to us when we learn from Herford that at the
time of the Maccabean revolt "the leading men of Jerusalem, or
many of them, were notoriously Hellenisers" and that therefore the
strength of the revolt lay with the common people.[42] The common
people, Herford thinks, "must have learned in some way to look
upon the Torah as containing the very essence of their religion." [43]
Was this the type of people who heard Jesus gladly? Did this people
somehow sense, as "common people" often do, that their leaders
were leaders who were directing them away from God? Were there
among this people many who, like Simeon and Anna in Jesus' day,
looked for the actual coming into their midst of the promised
Messiah? How could there be after about 250 years of teaching

74

by their rabbis according to the principles of the Unwritten Torah? By his sovereign grace the God of Abraham preserved a remnant for himself among his covenant-breaking people!

There were in this period "extreme devotees of the Torah," Hasidim. These were strong in their opposition to Hellenism. But why was this the case? Was it because of a true faith in the coming Messiah? Or was it merely because of a false nationalism such as marked many of the Jews in Jesus' day? How could we know? Among those who were "zealous for the Torah" there may have been both true believers and mere nationalists.[44]

When Mattathias gave the signal for revolt he used these words: "Whoso is zealous for the Torah, and would maintain the covenant, let him come forth after me." [45] In using these words he likely had in mind, says Herford, the curse under which Daniel said the people suffered because they had failed to observe the covenant.[46] But what did this mean? If they really meant what Daniel meant when he spoke of God's wrath, then they had to reject what their leaders, the followers of the Unwritten Torah, meant. For these latter the idea of the wrath of God could mean nothing more than such an idea would mean for the Greeks. For them God had become the unknowable one and the idea of a law of such an unknowable God was but a metaphorical or allegorical way of speaking about such an unknowable one.

Herford thinks that by referring to the Torah and its curse the nature of the Jewish revolt against Hellenism is made clear. Says he: "Such then was the nature of the resistance offered to Hellenism by the defenders of the Torah, and it only remains to indicate the character of the victory which they won." [47] Herford speaks of the "victory of the Torah over Hellenism." [48] But he adds that nationalism too may have had a part to play in this victory. Even so, he says, "the victory in question is the victory of the Torah over Hellenism," and he adds that this "victory was complete and final." [49] Summing up the whole matter, Herford says: "So far as the Jewish state was concerned, Hellenism was done with; and the Torah was henceforth acknowledged by all as the supreme religious authority, whatever interpretation might be put upon its precepts and its obligations, and whether or not the homage offered to it was sincere." [50]

The Torah, says Herford, "was acknowledged by everyone, by Sadducees no less than by Pharisees, by Zealots no less than by Essenes. It was only when these several parties came to apply their principles to practical objects that their divergent views of what the Torah was became apparent. All the types of Judaism represented by the various sects which arose after the Maccabean Revolt took their stand upon the Torah, and from their own point of view were entirely loyal to it." [51]

It was therefore, in the last analysis, not the temple but the Torah that served as a rallying point for Judaism. "To purify and re-dedicate the Temple was, however, only the symbol of the victory of Torah and the defeat of Hellenism." [52]

It is not difficult to see how, on such a view of the Torah, Martin Buber too can think himself as true to it and therefore to the Jewish principle. With the introduction of the Unwritten Torah, the floodgates were opened and Hellenism was in fact, though not in theory, victorious. All who believe in God as the unknowable and in his law as expressing the best and highest of what the reason and the conscience of apostate man can devise may now be thought of as being true Jews. "The teachers who introduced the conception of the Unwritten Torah, and thereby broke the connexion between the halachah and the written text, were quite aware of the extreme gravity of the step they were taking. They intended to modify the written commandment in various ways, and in course of time actually did so in numberless cases. Yet they had before them the plain injunction (Deut. iv. 2): 'Ye shall not add to the word which I command you, neither shall ye diminish from it; that ye may keep the commandments of the Lord your God which I command you.' Of course, a theory which justified a departure from the written word would justify a disregard of this particular written word; but the real justification of the procedure was 'that ye may keep the commandments of the Lord your God.' If the commandment could not be kept according to the strict letter, the true intention of the commandment could be fulfilled by departure from the letter. And, whatever was done by means of the Unwritten Torah to modify, or even abolish, the written word of a commandment, was always done for the purpose of fulfilling the real intention of the commandment, to make the Torah effective instead of letting it become obsolete because impracticable." [53]

76

The teachers of the Torah were constantly raising the ethical standards and reinterpreting the words of the Torah accordingly.[54] These teachers had their reasons for adjusting the words of the Torah. Such adjustment was made:

(a) Because of the needs of the time.

(b) For the adjustment of human relations.

(c) For the raising of the standard of religous and moral life.

(d) Because of human weakness.

(e) When the reason for a law no longer operates.[55]

Modern Protestantism as well as Roman Catholicism have been adept learners of these teachers of an Unwritten Torah. And such men as Buber have every right to call themselves defenders of the Torah even as they are, in fact, defenders of the modern idea of the primacy of the practical reason.

NOTES

1. R. Travers Herford, *Talmud and Apocrypha*, (London: The Soncino Press, 1933).

2. *Ibid.*, p. 3.

3. *Ibid.*

4. *Ibid.*, p. 9.

5. *Ibid.*, p. 11.

6. *Ibid.*

7. *Ibid.*, p. 12.

8. *Ibid.*, p. 14.

9. *Ibid.*, p. 24.

10. *Ibid.*, p. 29.

11. *Ibid.*, p. 36.

12. *Ibid.*, p. 43.

13. *Ibid.*

14. *Ibid.*, p. 44.

15. *Ibid.*, p. 46.

16. *Ibid.*

17. *Ibid.*, p. 47.

18. *Ibid.*, p. 50.

19. *Ibid.*, pp. 53-54.

20. *Ibid.*, p. 54.

21. *Ibid.*,

22. *Ibid.*, p. 55.

23. *Ibid.*, p. 56.

24. *Ibid.*, p. 57.
25. *Ibid.*, p. 63.
26. *Ibid.*, pp. 63-64.
27. *Ibid.*, p. 64.
28. *Ibid.*, p. 63.
29. *Ibid.*, p. 64 .
30. *Ibid.*, p. 65.
31. *Ibid.*, p. 66.
32. *Ibid.*
33. *Ibid.*, p. 66.
34. *Ibid.*, pp. 66-67.
35. *Ibid.*, p. 68.
36. *Ibid.*, pp. 68-69.
37. *Ibid.*, p. 71.
38. *Ibid.*
39. *Ibid.*, p. 72.
40. *Ibid.*
41. *Ibid.*, p. 73.
42. *Ibid.*, p. 80.
43. *Ibid.*
44. *Ibid.*, p. 84.
45. *Ibid.*, p. 85.
46. *Ibid.*, p. 86.
47. *Ibid.*
48. *Ibid.*
49. *Ibid.*, p. 87.
50. *Ibid.*
51. *Ibid.*, pp. 87-88.
52. *Ibid.*, p. 88.
53. *Ibid.*, pp. 113-114.
54. *Ibid.*, p. 116.
55. *Ibid.*, p. 117.

CHAPTER IV

THE LORD OF HISTORY

In the previous chapter it was our concern to understand the Jewish conception of Torah. This was the question of God's revelation to man and of man's response to this revelation. It was, in short, the question of epistemology. In the present chapter it will be our concern to understand the Jewish conception of God's control of history and of man's response to this control. This is, in short, the question of metaphysics.

As was the case in the previous chapter, we shall deal only with the general picture. There we sought to discover the nature of *normative* Judaism. In this final chapter we seek to discover the nature of *catholic* Judaism. Of course, normative and catholic Judaism are involved in one another.

In our search we shall, to begin with, follow K. Kohler's work on *Jewish Theology*.[1] Says Kohler: "Jewish theology differs radically from Christian theology in the following three points:

"A. The theology of Christianity deals with articles of faith formulated by the founders and heads of the Church as conditions of *salvation,* so that any alteration in favor of free thought threatens to undermine the very plan of salvation upon which the Church was founded. Judaism recognizes only such articles of faith as were adopted by the people voluntarily as expressions of their religious consciousness, both without external compulsion and without doing violence to the dictates of reason. Judaism does not know salvation by faith in the sense of Paul, the real founder of the Church, who declared the blind acceptance of belief to be in itself meritorious. It denies the existence of any irreconcilable opposition between faith and reason.

"B. Christian theology rests upon a *formula of confession,* the so-called Symbolum of the Apostolic Church, which alone makes one a Christian. Judaism has no such formula of confession which renders a Jew a Jew. No ecclesiastical authority ever dictated or regulated the belief of a Jew; his faith has been voiced in the solemn liturgical form of prayer, and has ever retained its freshness and vigor of thought in the consciousness of the people. This partly accounts for the antipathy toward any kind of dogma or creed among Jews.

"C. The creed is a *conditio sine qua non* of the Christian Church. To disbelieve its dogmas is to cut oneself loose from membership. Judaism is quite different. The Jew is *born* into it and cannot extricate himself from it even by the renunciation of his faith, which would but render him an apostate Jew. This condition exists, because the racial community formed, and still forms, the basis of the religious community. It is birth, not confession, that imposes on the Jew the obligation to work and strive for the eternal verities of Israel, for the preservation and propagation of which he has been chosen by the God of history." [2]

The aim of Judaism, says Kohler, "is not so much the salvation of the soul in the hereafter as the salvation of humanity in history." [3]

Can we then really speak of the "essence of Judaism"? Kohler thinks we can. Says he: "There can be no disputing the fact that the central idea of Judaism and its life purpose is the doctrine of the One Only and Holy God, whose kindom of truth, justice and peace is to be universally established at the end of time. This is the main teaching of Scripture and the hope voiced in the liturgy; while Isreal's mission to defend, to unfold and to propagate this truth is a corollary of the doctrine itself and cannot be separated from it. Whether we regard it as Law or a system of doctrine, as religious truth or world-mission, this belief pledged the little tribe of Judah to a warfare of many thousands of years against the hordes of heathendom with all their idolatry and brutality, their deification of man and their degradation of deity to human rank. It betokened a battle for the pure idea of God and man, which is not to end until the principle of divine holiness has done away with every form of life that tends to degrade and to disunite mankind, and until Israel's Only One has become the unifying power and the highest ideal of all humanity." [4]

80

If then we think of Judaism we must think, to be sure, of the nation of Israel and we must think of its ritual. But we must also, and at the same time, think of the "great world-duty of Israel." [5] How far wrong we would be in thinking of the Jewish nation as slavishly obedient to an externally promulgated law. Their law is the product of their religious consciousness. This being the case the ritual of the law does not indicate a narrow and mechanical legalism but a means by which the religious consciousness seeks to order the whole life of man around one center, namely the glory of God. Again, since the religious consciousness is the ultimate organizing principle of life then the final aim of man is the "salvation" of mankind. We must, therefore, not speak of "a 'Mosaic,' 'Hebrew,' or 'Israelitish' religion." Judaism "points back to the patriarchs as its first source of revelation. It speaks not of the God of Moses, of Amos and Isaiah, but of the God of Abraham, Isaac, and Jacob, thereby declaring the Jewish genius to be the creator of its own religious ideas." [6]

Did not God promise Abraham that his seed should be the source of great blessing to the world? We can see how this blessing has been fulfilled, to a large extent, even through Christianity and Mohammedanism. The prophet Zechariah expressed the world-wide significance of the seed of Abraham in these words: "It shall come to pass on that day that living waters shall go out from Jerusalem; half of them toward the eastern sea and half of them toward the western sea. . . . And the Lord shall be King over all the earth; in that day shall the Lord be One, and His name one." [7]

"The prophetic words of Zechariah," says Kohler, "may be applied to the two great world-religions which emanated from Judaism and won fully half of the human race, as it exists at present, for the God of Abraham. Though they have incorporated many non-Jewish elements in their systems, they have spread the fundamental truths of the Jewish faith and Jewish ethics to every part of the earth. Christianity in the West and Islam in the East have aided in leading mankind ever nearer to the pure monotheistic truth. Consciously or unconsciously, both found their guiding motive in the Messianic hope of the prophets of Israel and based their moral systems on the ethics of the Hebrew Scriptures. The leading spirits of Judaism recognized this, declaring both the Christian and Mohammedan religions to be agencies of Divine Providence, intrusted with the historical mission of cooperating in the building up of the Messianic Kingdom, thus preparing for the ultimate triumph of pure monotheism in the hearts and lives of all men and nations of the world." [8]

We shall therefore no longer think of Judaism "as a nomistic religion, caring only for the external observance of the Law." [9] We must seek for the inwardness of principle that lies behind all the detailed questions of law with which Judaism concerned itself.

When, for instance, we read Louis Finklestein's life of Akiba (Philadelphia, 1936) we may at first think it odd and artificial when he attaches special significance to the word *lemor* "which in biblical Hebrew always introduces direct discourse." But we must not "accept at their face value the technical reasons he gives for his decision" with respect to points of biblical exegesis. If we did so we would think of him as a "brilliant example of extraordinary—but wasted ingenuity."

We must realize, however, that "the greatest of talmudists . . . considered the interpretation of the written law" to be "merely a form which had to be followed in the derivation of desirable rules from the Scriptural text. The "rules which he derives through his curious and intricate logic are so reasonable that when we examine them we are even more impressed with his judgment as a juirst, than with his skill as a debator" (p. 171).

I. Idolatry

If it is the religious consciousness in general and the Jewish genius in particular that originates the ideal religion of mankind, namely, the service of the one true God, then all forms of idolatry must be rejected. This means that the "dualistic and trinitarian beliefs of other religions" must be rejected. It is the "doctrine of God's unity," strengthened as it is by its rejection of dualism and trinitarianism, that gives "lucidity and sublimity" to the Jewish point of view. "The Jewish conception of God thus makes *truth,* as well as *righteousness* and *love,* both a moral duty for man and a historical task comprising all humanity." [10]

It is the task of "progressive Judaism" to re-emphasize Israel's world-mission "and to reclaim for Judaism its place as the priesthood of humanity." [11] Israel, as the people of the covenant, aims to unite all nations and classes of men in the divine covenant. It must outlast all other religions in its certainty that ultimately there can be but one religion, uniting God and man by a single bond." [12] "Judaism centers upon its sublime and simple conception of God. This lifts it above all other religions and satisfies in unique measure the longing for truth and inner peace amidst the futility and incessant changes of earthly existence." [13]

It goes without saying that if Judaism is what Kohler says it is, then it cannot tolerate the Christian teaching of the incarnation any more than it can tolerate the Christian doctrine of the trinity. The Jews of Jesus' day were consantly charging Jesus with blasphemy. What else could they do since, from their point of view, God *cannot* be incarnate? The question was not, finally, whether some other man, rather than Jesus, was the promised Messiah. The question ultimately pertained to the nature of the Messiah. The "pure" monotheism of the Jews of Jesus' day did not allow even for the *possibility* of *any man* to be the Son of God, with the right to claim that he was one with the Father.

How then can the world-wide mission of Judaism be accomplished? Does not idolatry, the service and worship of man, abound in the earth? And does not Christianity, following the Apostle Paul in his elevation of Jesus to the level of identity with God, present the most difficult problem for Judaism? We have heard Kohler say that "Christianity in the West and Islam in the East have aided in leading mankind ever nearer to the pure monotheistic truth." [14] But we ask Kohler, how can this be? Is not the idea of the incarnate Christ as the Son of God and son of man the *center* of the Christian religion? Christianity claims that no one knows God truly as Father except through him. There is no point to setting Jesus and Paul over against one another on this point. Paul simply set forth in its full significance the fact that Jesus was the Son of God, as he claimed to be. And further, it is the divinity of Jesus by which Christianity seeks always and alone to bring men to God. Kohler and his fellow-Jews undoubtedly hold that Christianity has, throughout the ages, been radically and fatally mistaken in their estimate of Jesus as the Son of God. Surely, then, if humanity is ever to reach "the pure monotheistic truth," then Christianity must reverse itself in its historic estimate of Jesus. The worship of Jesus Christ as God is, from the Jewish point of view, pure idolatry. Christians must be converted

83

from this idolatry if they are to join humanity in the worship of the one true God.

But we have all the while spoken of historic or orthodox Christianity, the Christianity of the historic Christian creeds. Perhaps it is quite hopeless to seek to win the adherents of these historic Christian creeds to the "pure monotheism" of the Jew. The believers in the historic creeds are themselves seeking to convert the Jews to their position. These orthodox Christians seek to convert all men, Jew as well as Gentile, Orthodox and Conservative as well as Reform Jews, to Jesus Christ as God and as Savior from sin. Without conversion to Jesus as God, these historic Christians hold, men are and remain forever under the wrath of God.

It is well then that the issue be clearly seen for what it is. Jews seek to convert Christians from their idolatry, their worship of a man, namely Jesus, as God. If men are to be "saved" they must, if they are Christians, renounce Christ as Son of God. On the other hand, Christians seek to convert the Jews from their idolatry, their service of a god of their own construction, their service of man. According to Christians, the "pure" monotheism of the Jew is but a cover-up for the worship of man.

II. The Jewish Principle and Modern Protestantism

At the moment the followers of the Jewish principle may be greatly encouraged by a basic rift among those who call themselves Christians. We refer to the difference between the followers of the historic Christian creeds and the followers of Immanuel Kant. The followers of Kant are in basic agreement with the Jewish principle of progressive revelation. The followers of Kant agree with the Jews when they assert that it is on the religious and moral consciousness of man that the source of all teaching with respect to the relation of God to man must be found.

We shall, for convenience, speak of the followers of Kant as new Protestants. The new Protestant, like the Pharisee, has a new hermeneutic. The Pharisee spoke highly of Moses as God's spokesman to man but in his idea of the Unwritten Torah he made his own moral consciousness the ultimate source of the knowledge between right and wrong. So too, the new-Protestant speaks highly of Christ but only because he is the projection of his religious and moral consciousness.

84

It is no wonder then that a man like Martin Buber finds an essential unity between the Jewish principle and the new-Protestant principle. And it is no wonder that he already sees the vision of a new community in which Jews and new Protestants give one another the kiss of brotherhood and from which only "fundamentalists" are excluded.

In this new community there need be no need for proselytizing. Every variety of theology may be tolerated so long as it is not idolatrous. And the only theology that is idolatrous is the theology of orthodox Protestants. Orthodox Christian theology alone holds that Jesus Christ, as he walked in Palestine, is one with God the Father.

To be sure, the new Protestant also speaks of Jesus as being one with God. In fact, new Protestantism claims to do far better justice to the idea of the identification of Jesus with God than orthodox theology does. According to new Protestantism the orthodox Christian view of Christ is docetic. Orthodox Christianity, we are told, does not really allow God to come into the state and fate of man. Orthodox theology, we are told, seeks to safeguard Jesus from pollution by contact with empirical man by speaking of the sinlessness of Jesus. Why do the orthodox not dare to say that God is wholly revealed in Jesus? They are afraid of bringing God down to the level of man. But they would have no need to be afraid of this if only they would say that God is wholly revealed in man and as such is wholly hidden in man. Then they would safeguard at one stroke the true transcendence and the true immanence of God.

No Jew desires to call us Christians idolatrous if only we safeguard the true dialectical character of God's relation to man, and it is this that Kant has helped us to do. Kant has helped us to see that any intellectual proposition that we may make about God is tantamount to making graven image of him. Kant has cured us Christians from idolatry in the way that Ezra cured the Jews from idolatry. The Jews know that what Moses said has its final source and norm in the ethical consciousness of man. The modern Christian knows that what Jesus said has its source and norm in the ethical consciousness of man.

III. Holiness and Glory

In the ultimacy of man's moral consciousness the new Protestant

85

and the Jew alike find the source of the true God-man relation. The "course of early Hebrew thinking" says Israel I. Efros, "was not from monotheism to ethics, but just the reverse, from ethics to monotheism. It is not that God is one and therefore ethical, but ethical—the absolutely ethical—and therefore one, for two kinds of morality would constitute relativity." [15] "God is ethics, and ethics—as an abstract absolute—is God." "And we should note here that this concept of God as abstract morality, as pure ethicalness, as that mystery of contradiction involved in an identity of value with being, constitutes the core of biblical ethics and contains an answer to many problems and difficulties." [17]

Which problems and difficulties are answered by this idea of God as the purely ethical? Efros does not discuss them in this connection. But it is obvious what he had in mind. It is the problem of man's freedom in relation to God's control over him and his world. Orthodox Christianity still struggles with this problem. There are Calvinists and there are Arminians among them. And the Roman Catholics have not altogether escaped the dilemma involved in the necessity-freedom problem. But the Jews as well as the modern Protestants have found true unity in God, true monotheism, by starting with the ethical consciousness of man as autonomous. It is this autonomous ethical consciousness that postulates the true unity because of the pure goodness of God.

What has been said so far about God stresses his holiness. In a sense the "whole course of Jewish thought became an incessant effort toward an evermore precise definition of God's spirituality, that is, toward an ever higher transcendence." [18] But "developing along with this process of sublimation, there was also the opposite tendency to bring the deity back into the world, a tendency born out of the longing for nearness and for a responsiveness to our cries of distress." [19]

There is, therefore, says Efros, "a great difference between the biblical God-concept and the *agathos* which is the highest idea in the Platonic system. *Agathos* exists for itself, sheds light out of itself upon itself, and is entirely passive with reference to the world, for, as stated in the beginning of this work, the elements of work and doing never entered into Greek theological meditation. The Greeks were ashamed of doing, so that in the frame of Hebraic activistic thinking, one cannot regard *agathos* as a god at all. But the Hebraic

86

God creates and does all; in all his nature he is interested and involved in all human doings, as he is absolute morality. He knocks, in a manner not found in any other literature, on all the windows of man; know me, recognize me, admit me! Why is he so interested to be known? Now it is clear. The transcendentally ethical longs by his very nature to clothe himself in human acts and relations because these constitute his concrete existence and meaning. It is out of this divine longing for reality that the various parts of doctrinal theology flow, for such a God must create a world to serve as a field of operation for his ethicalness. So, from God's standpoint, he is *eternally* a creator of time. And he must reveal himself, because without a Mount Sinai, the sun is blind, i.e., without beams. And he is always provident and watchful; unlike the Platonic *agathos* and Aristotle's pure Form, he is a "God of seeing" (Gen. 16:13). Hence, God has a necessary function in the life of man. He is not an intruder into our little world, making laws for us to obey. He is invited by our suffering. The outcry calls into the I AM. His laws of mercy and goodness are our quest and our own legislation. Man needs God who needs man. Otherwise, the God of Israel would have long flown away and vanished in the wide heavens of methphysics. Perhaps this is what happened to Buddhism. Man and God are tied to each other unto eternity. 'Thou hast avouched the Lord this day . . . and the Lord has avouched thee' (Deut. 26:17-18). The ethical absolute is therefore both transcendent and immanent, so that the two schools of biblical thought, Holiness and Glory, here coalesce and are one." [20]

IV. The Origin and Destiny of Man

The Jewish notion of man corresponds to the Jewish notion of God. But what more need be said on this subject? By implication all has been said that needs to be said. If the transcendentally ethical longs "to clothe himself in human acts and relations because these constitute his concrete existence and meaning" [21] then man, as well as God, must say, "I *act,* and therefore I am." [22]

God is the great *I am.* As such he is "the subject of the world." [23] And man is able to say, I *act,* therefore I am, because man in acting attains unity with God. Knowledge of God, "which in the Bible means ethical knowledge, is a union of the human I with the divine I, so that for the space of a moment man becomes God and gives unto himself moral laws." [24]

It is only this moral-metaphysical self-identification, as God is ethics itself, that provides us with that Kantian autonomy, morality for the sake of morality, which alone constitutes a moral act, for it never moves out of the ethical sphere and therefore ceases to be obedience and becomes self-legislation. Thus the moral choice is a mystic union expressible in the formula I-I, and it leaves, like all mystic experiences, a strangely happy feeling in its wake. It is a feeling of conquest of separation and aloneness, and it constitutes a return to primeval oneness with the All.

"There is then a basic difference between psychological self-searching and an ethical experience. When I observe myself, my self, psychologically, I become an object to myself, losing my self under the very beam of self-inspection, and the effort fails. Ethically, however, I join the cosmic I, forming an I-I, so that I am again my subject, only with wider reaches and metaphysical implications. I become my own moral legislator, for it is only a free self that can legislate moral laws, but all objects are bound and determined by the thinking object. Hence, the moral self is the religious self, a conscious spark of a great flame: Thus said the Lord. The moment of ethical crisis is therefore a mystical experience." [25]

"What then," asks Efros, "is the source and sanction of biblical ethics?" His answer is: "Not the dictates of reason in quest of happiness, but the hearing of the 'I am the Lord' in the voice of the categorical imperative, an intuitive knowledge of the good as a self-revelation and concretization of the Absolute Good, a correlation of the individual deed with the Infinite which thus confers upon the deed and upon man metaphysical implications. Is biblical ethics then religious, or, if counterpoint it be, autonomous? Certainly religious, because it springs from God and in its effectiveness returns unto Him; but since God Himself is conceived as value-being, that is, in no other terms than pure ethicalness, the source and sanction operates within the ethical sphere and is therefore internal, autonomous." [26]

The evidence is overwhelming that the ethicalisms of the Jewish and of the Kantian philosophies are, to all intents and purposes, identical. It remains only to point out that Efros is mistaken when he sees a gulf opening up between Israel and Greece. It is, he says, "the gulf of Greek intellectualism." [27] Many writers would see the same gulf between the Greek view and that of Kant's primacy of the practical reason. On inspection the "great gulf" turns out to be a mirage.

In the first place, there is the same starting point for Jewish, Greek, and Kantian ethics, namely, the autonomy of man's ethical consciousness. All three positions look for a "pure monotheism" by means of postulating the idea of the "good" as above all intellectual statements that man can make about it.

In the second place, the god of all three positions is, accordingly, the god of pure negation.

In the third place, all three positions seek for contact between man and God by means of pure mysticism. The "moral self," says Efros, "is the religious self, a conscious spark of a great flame: Thus saith the Lord. The moment of ethical crisis is therefore a mystical experience." [28] The origin and destiny of man is, accordingly, in all three positions essentially the same. In all three cases man's moral consciousness sets up ideals for itself which it speaks of as commandments that come from God. When man does not live up to the moral ideals that he has cast up for himself then he threatens himself with his disapproval which he speaks of as the wrath of God. Meanwhile he keeps encouraging himself by speaking of the ideal state, the kingdom of righteousness, the kingdom of heaven which the holy but all-merciful God will establish with man's help. "Some great one," a "Messiah" or a series of Messiahs may help forward the coming of the millennium. But the millennium will always be ahead of any actually existent state of affairs. "The problem of human destiny is answered by Judaism," says Kohler, "with the idea that God is the ideal and pattern of all morality." [29]

V. Sin

The fact of sin does not, according to Judaism, stop man from approaching the ideal of the kingdom of God. "Judaism rejects completely the belief in hereditary sin and the corruption of the flesh." [30] "Therefore the pious Jew begins his daily prayer with the words: 'My God, the soul which thou hast given me is pure.'" [31] "In fact, the whole Paradise story could never be made the basis for a dogma. The historicity of the serpent is denied by Saadia;

the rabbis transfer Paradise with the tree of life to heaven as a reward for the future; and both Nahmanides the mystic and Maimonides the philosopher give it an allegorical meaning." [32]

"The 'book of the generation of man' which begins with Adam is accordingly not the history of man's descent, but of his continuous ascent, of ever higher achievements and aspirations; it is not a record of the fall of man, but of his rise from age to age." [33]

Judaism has, accordingly, "ever emphasized the freedom of the will as one of its chief doctrines. The dignity and greatness of man depends largely upon his freedom, his power of self-determination. He differs from the lower animals in his independence of instinct as the dictator of his actions." [34]

To be sure, Kohler speaks of sin as an "offense against God, provoking His punishment." [35] No man "is sinful by nature," but "as man has a nature of flesh, which is sensuous and selfish, each person is inclined to sin and none is perfectly free from it." [36]

Of course, argues Kohler, this "high," personal view of sin was a matter of historical development. During the "dominance of the priestly view the gravest possible offense was one against the cult. . . ." [37] But "the more the prophetic conception of the moral nature of the Deity permeated the Jewish religion, the more the term sin came to mean an offense against the holiness of God, the Guardian of morality. Hence the great prophets upbraided the people for their moral, not their ceremonial failings." [38] "The only ritual offenses emphasized [by the prophets] as sins against God are idolatry, violation of the name of God and of the Sabbath, for these express the sanctity of life." [39] Samuel anticipated this view when he said: "Behold, to obey is better than sacrifice. . . ." [40]

Summing it all up, Kohler says: "At any rate, Judaism recognizes no sin which does not arise from the individual conscience or moral personality." [41]

It is sin, as thus personalistically conceived, that "contaminates man, so that he cannot stand in the presence of God. The holiness of Him who is, 'of eyes too pure to behold evil' becomes to the sinner 'a devouring fire.' " [42] Conscious of sin in this deep personal sense, Isaiah knew that he "must undergo atonement in order to be prepared for his high prophetic task." [43]

In all this we are still on the high ethical plateau of which we have heard Efros speak so fully. And the main point of the ethical

90

view as Efros described it lies, of course, in the fact that man, in effect, becomes God and gives laws to himself. Accordingly, sin, as fully personalistic, brings man face to face with the holiness of God, but this holiness of God is the projection of man's moral ideals.

Thus the "pure monotheism" of the Jewish position requires not only "pure" negative theology but also a symbolical or mythological theology. When God is constantly said to be personal, this is merely the hypostatization of an ideal.

VI. Atonement

Because of this view of man and his sin it is not surprising to hear Kohler say: "The Jewish idea of atonement by the sinner's return to God excludes every kind of mediatorship. Neither the priesthood nor sacrifice is necessary to secure the divine grace; man need only find the way to God by his own efforts. 'Seek ye Me, and live,' says God to His erring children.

"*Teshubah,* which means return, is an idea peculiar to Judaism, created by the prophets of Israel, and arising directly from the simple Jewish conception of sin. Since sin is a deviation from the path of salvation, a 'straying' into the road of perdition and death, the erring can return with heart and soul, end his ways, and thus change his entire being." [44]

In all this the idea of *inwardness* is central. The law of God addressing man is man's high moral consciousness addressing itself. Sin against the law is failure of the moral self to live up to its own ideals. Atonement for this sin against one's own moral ideal involves "an inner change, a transformation of soul, renewing both heart and spirit." [45] This is repentance and repentance is atonement.

Sin did not come into the world by the willful transgression of Adam at the beginning of history. Sin cannot be removed from the heart of man through anything that happens for man by a mediator removed from him by time and place. The entire transition from wrath to grace is an internal process within the moral consciousness of man. "Judaism considers sin merely moral aberration, not utter corruption, and believes in the capability of the very worst of sinners to improve his ways; therefore it waits ever for his regeneration. This is truly a return to God, the restoration of the divine image which has been disfigured and corrupted by sin." [46]

91

The idea of universal salvation follows from the principle of inwardness described. Says Kohler: "Rabbi Akiba probably referred to the Paulinian dogma that Jesus, the crucified Messiah, is the only son of God, in his well-known saying: 'Beloved is man, for he is created in God's image, and it was a special token of love that he became conscious of it. Beloved is Israel, for they are called the children of God, and it was a special token of love that they became conscious of it.' Here he claims the glory of being a son of God for Israel, but not for all men. Still, as soon as the likeness of man to God is taken in a spiritual sense, then it is implied that all men have the same capacity for being a son of God which is claimed for Israel. This is unquestionably the view of Judaism when it considers the Torah as entrusted to Israel to bring light and blessing to all the families of men." [47]

We do well at this point to reflect afresh on the great similarity or virtual identity of the Jewish and modern Protestant view of ethical inwardness. If Rabbi Akiba did allude to Jesus, as Kohler thinks he did, then he was extremely courteous and gracious. We have heard the gracious words about Jesus spoken by Martin Buber. However, there is not the least doubt but that Akiba and Buber, as well as Judaism in general, remove Jesus and his work of atonement from the scene. Jesus and his atonement for sinners constitutes to them a declaration of war to the death on their notion of ethical inwardness. Jesus and his atonement constitutes to them an attack on their self-righteousness. How can anyone be righteous, really righteous, if it is not he himself who seeks righteousness?

The Jew today therefore makes grateful use of the principle of ethical autonomy as developed by Kant. The modern Protestants are now his allies in the defense of the inwardness of the principle of sin and atonement. The modern Protestant is, if possible, more courteous than are the Jews. Even so, they as well as the Jew crucify the Son of God afresh. Has not Kant taught them that such moral transactions as sin and atonement cannot, in the nature of the case, take place in the I-it dimension? Surely, they argue, if sin and atonement are to have genuine meaning for us, the meaning must be that they take place in the person-to-person dimension. Here is, on this view, true inwardness..

Thus it appears anew that the modern Protestant need send no missionaries to the Jews. There is nothing the new Protestant can tell the Jew. Similarly, there is nothing the Jew need tell the new Protestant. They are friends and brothers in common opposition to those who believe in man's sin and in atonement as centering in Jesus Christ as historical. Those Presbyterians who received the *Confession of 1967* are relieved of responsibility to the Jews.

VII. The Kingdom of Heaven

Everything that has been said so far in this chapter is calculated to lead toward an understanding of the Jewish philosophy of history. We have seen that the idea of the unity of God, the oneness of God is based, not on metaphysical speculation, but on the autonomy of man's moral consciousness.

The same centrality of the ethical consciousness, in postulating the oneness of God, also postulates his victory over all evil. It was the centrality of the ethical consciousness that led the Jews to the "historical conception of the world." [48] Perhaps we might turn this about and say that their discovery of the historical character of the world led them to the idea that "the Jewish religion was intended to become the religion of the whole world." [49]

But if this is to be the case then the Jew must feel the command within him "to go out to all mankind." The idea of mission is "essential to a true religion." [50] The Jews knew "that Judaism spoke to all men of the innermost aspect of human existence." [51] "Abraham received the promise and exhortation. In thee shall all the families of the earth be blessed." [52] Judaism has never abandoned the claim to be the world religion. Were it not replete with the consciousness of this ideal, its whole history would seem petty and even incomprehensible." [53]

Now the message which Judaism brings to the world and by which the world alone is to be saved is the message of "ethical optimism." [54] "The belief that there is meaning in all things is possible only as a belief in the good." [55] Belief in the good is based on belief in God as transcendent above the world of causality—the world of science. Belief in the good and belief in God is not only beyond the reach of science but also beyond the reach of philosophy. It is not by systematizing the accumulated facts of experience but by religious and ethical experience that we believe in God. "Religion measures man's experience in terms of its intrinsic values, and

93

thereby it is able to go beneath the surface of existence to apprehend its inner core." [56]

The good "demands an unconditional, absolute foundation. Its basis can therefore be found only in the One God, the outcome of whose nature is the moral law. In him the good finds the certainty of its eternal reality. And thus the good arises from the source of all existence: its law emerges from the depth in which the secret is contained. The One God is the answer to all mystery; he is the source of all that is eternal and ethical, creative and ordered, hidden and definite. From this alliance between the secret and the commandment issues all existence and all significance." [57]

Since then Judaism alone has seen this vision of the "alliance between the secret and the commandment"; its world-wide mission is therewith clear. And, happily, the message of ethical optimism is bound to find response everywhere. All men already possess the ethical consciousness. And all men have, therefore, also the ability to work toward the realization of the ethical ideal. "The optimism of Judaism consists of the belief in God, and consequently also a belief in man, who is able to realize in himself the good which first finds its reality in God. From the optimism all the ideas of Judaism can be derived. Thereby a threefold relationship is established. First, the belief in oneself: one's soul is created in the image of God and is therefore capable of purity and freedom; the soul is the arena in which reconciliation with God is always possible. Secondly, the belief in one's neighbor: every human being has the same individuality that I have; his soul with its possible purity and freedom also derives from God; and he is at bottom akin to me and is therefore my neighbor and brother. Thirdly, the belief in mankind: all men are children of God; hence they are welded together by a common task. To know the spiritual reality of one's own life, of the life of our neighbors and of the life of humanity as a whole as they are grounded in the common reality of God—this is the expression of Jewish optimism." [58]

It should be noted that this ethical optimism of which Baeck speaks as being the "essence of Judaism" excludes what he speaks of as mythology. Baeck's view of ethical monotheism is, to all intents and purposes, the same as that of Efros (cf. pp. 64-66). Inherent in this notion of ethical monotheism and that of ethical optimism is the idea that it *cannot* exclude any human being. To

94

be sure, sin is opposed to the realization of the kingdom of heaven. But atonement for sin is within reach of every man. It is not within reach of every man because of the fact that every man in all the world has heard about Judaism. Rather, it is within the reach of every man, because to be man at all, one is conscious of the difference between good and evil and because atonement for sin is a "free ethical deed" that every man can accomplish.[59]

Of course this vision of ethical optimism was a gradual growth even in Judaism. It was only gradually that Judaism saw the need of stepping out of the Temple, "the forecourt of life, into real life." But with the prophetic vision of ethical monotheism "atonement and repentance" entered "into their innermost sanctuary, the human heart. Thus Judaism was able to divest itself of the sacrificial service without substituting any sacrament or mystery." [60]

It is the "messianic idea" that expresses this great unity, this exclusion of all exclusiveness. This messianic idea, based as it is on the autonomy of the ethical self-consciousness, therefore, excludes Christianity. Christianity is said to be mythological. It brings the ethical relation between God and man down to the level of the causal dimension of science and to the theoretical dimension of philosophy. For this reason Christianity holds that the Messiah must be identified with Jesus of Nazareth who has accomplished salvation for his people. Over against this view of Christianity and of the Messiah as identified with the historical Jesus "Judaism stresses the kingdom of God not as something already accomplished but as something yet to be achieved, not as a religious possession of the elect but as the moral task of all. In Judaism man sanctifies the world by sanctifying God and by overcoming evil and realizing good. The kingdom of God lies before him because it lies before all. For Judaism, the whole of mankind is chosen; God's covenant was made with all men. And finally Judaism maintains that man's creed is that he believes in God, and therefore in mankind, but not that he believes in a creed." [61]

In particular the Christian idea of grace must be rejected. Instead of looking to Jesus as the one God-man for salvation and allowing him to do the work of redemption for man, we must set man himself to work. "For Judaism the kingdom of God is not a kingdom above the world or opposed to it or even side by side with it. Rather is it the answer to the world given by man's goal:

95

the reconciliation of the world's finiteness with its infinity. It is not a future of miracle for which man can only wait, but a future of commandment which always has its present and ever demands a beginning and decision from man. In its idea lies the knowledge that man is a creative being, the contradiction of the conception that he remains bound and confined in the doom of guilt which only a miracle can break. To Judaism the kingdom of God is something which man, as the Rabbis say, 'takes upon himself.' Man must choose this kingdom. It is the kingdom of piety into which man enters through the moral service of God, through the conviction that the divine will is not something foreign to him or parallel to his life but the fulfilment of his days. He who knows and acknowledges God through never ending good deeds is on the road to the kingdom of God." [62]

Who then is the Lord of history? According to Judaism it is the God of ethical monotheism. This God is indistinguishable from the God of post-Kantian liberal-dialectic theology. In both Judaism and modern Protestant theology it is the principle of inwardness of the self-sufficient moral consciousness that postulates the existence of this God. Not that this God is manifest in any way in the facts of science or in the reasoning processes of men. The God of both Judaism and modern Protestantism is the wholly unknown and wholly unknowable one.

How then can this unknowable God be known to bring about the victory of good over evil? And how then can this unknowable God tell man of the difference even between good and evil?

The answer is clear. It is the moral consciousness in itself and by itself that makes the distinction between good and evil and that asserts that what it calls good will be victorious over what it says is evil.

Baeck says that "there are but two fundamental and determining forms of religion, that of Israel and that of Buddha. The former declares the world to be the field of life's tasks and offers a moral affirmation of the value of man's relationship to the world by deed and will; the latter declares that man's task is to devote himself to self-meditation without the exercise of his volition. The one is the expression of the command to work and create, the other of the need to rest." [63]

96

It is clear, however, that there is a deeper cleavage than that between Judaism and Buddhism. The question is not that between a religion of action and religion of rest. The question is rather between a religion based on the self-sufficiency of fallen man and a religion based on the revelation of God's grace to sinners in Christ.

Judaism naturally speaks much of its guardianship of the oracles of God with respect to man and his Creator-Redeemer. But by its unwillingness to see that Moses and the prophets spoke of Jesus as the Christ, Judaism has hardened itself in apostacy.

The principle of inwardness of which modern Judaism speaks so much is but an accommodation to the principle of inwardness by which modern Protestantism speaks. Judaism uses its principle of ethical monotheism as a means by which to stifle the voice of prophecy and thus indirectly to silence the claim of Christ. Modern Protestantism uses the same principle of ethical monotheism as a means by which to substitute a false Christ for the Christ of the New Testament.

When Jesus says that all power is given to him by the Father in view of his death and resurrection, and that he will vanquish the last enemy which is death, the modern Jew and the modern Protestant consider this mythology. The modern Jew will gladly join the modern Protestant in speaking of Christ as a Messiah if only the messianic idea be demythologized by means of the self-sufficient ethical consciousness. The modern Protestant theologian is ready and eager to oblige the modern Jew. The Protestant church is ready and eager to follow both, as the *Confession of 1967* illustrates.

If the true Christ is to be presented to men, evangelical Christians must, with Paul, beseech the Jew really to repent from sin, to repent not in the strength of a righteousness that he has within himself but in the strength of the righteousness that God has in Christ given unto men.

NOTES

1. K. Kohler, *Jewish Theology* (New York: The MacMillan Company, 1923).
2. *Ibid.*, pp. 5-6.
3. *Ibid.*, p. 6.
4. *Ibid.*, p. 15.

5. *Ibid.*, p. 16.
6. *Ibid.*
7. *Ibid.*, p. 426.
8. *Ibid.*
9. *Ibid.*, p. 13.
10. Kohler, *op. cit.*, p. 23.
11. *Ibid.*, p. 51.
12. *Ibid.*
13. *Ibid.*, p. 52.
14. *Op. Cit.*, p. 426.
15. Israel I. Efros, *Ancient Jewish Philosophy* (Detroit: Wayne State University Press, 1964), p. 84.
16. *Ibid.*
17. *Ibid.*, p. 85.
18. *Ibid.*, p. 8.
19. *Ibid.*, p. 9.
20. *Ibid.*, p. 85.
21. *Ibid.*
22. *Ibid.*, p. 86.
23. *Ibid.*
24. *Ibid.*, p. 87.
25. *Ibid.*
26. *Ibid.*, p. 90.
27. *Ibid.*, p. 87.
28. *Ibid.*
29. Kohler, *op. cit.*, p. 218.
30. *Ibid.*, p. 223.
31. *Ibid.*
32. *Ibid.*, p. 224.
33. *Ibid.*, p. 225.
34. *Ibid.*, p. 231.
35. *Ibid.*, p. 238.
36. *Ibid.*, pp. 239-240.
37. *Ibid.*, p. 241.
38. *Ibid.*
39. *Ibid.*
40. *Ibid.*
41. *Ibid.*, p. 243.
42. *Ibid.*, p. 244.
43. *Ibid.*
44. *Ibid.*, p. 247.
45. *Ibid.*
46. *Ibid.*, p. 248.
47. *Ibid.*, pp. 259-260.
48. Leo Baeck, *The Essence of Judaism* (New York: Schocken Books,

Inc., 1948), p. 76.

49. *Ibid.*
50. *Ibid.*, p. 77.
51. *Ibid.*
52. *Ibid.*, pp. 77-78.
53. *Ibid.*, p. 79.
54. *Ibid.*, p. 84.
55. *Ibid.*
56. *Ibid.*, p. 83.
57. *Ibid.*, p. 84.
58. *Ibid.*, p. 87.
59. *Ibid.*, p. 59.
60. *Ibid.*
61. *Ibid.*, p. 252.
62. *Ibid.*, p. 243.
63. *Ibid.*, p. 60.